DELFTWARE
Faience Production at Delft

H.-P. Fourest

DELFTWARE
Faience Production at Delft

Translated by Katherine Watson

Setting: Arts graphiques Les Remparts SA, Yverdon
Printing: Imprimeries Réunies SA, Lausanne
Photolithographs (colour): Cooperativa lavoratori grafici, Verona
(black and white): Atesa Argraf SA, Geneva
Binding: Mayer & Souter SA, Renens
Editorial: Barbara Perroud
Design: André Rosselet
Production: Marcel Berger
Photo Research: Ingrid de Kalbermatten

Translated from the French, *La Faïence de Delft*
French-language edition:
© 1980, Office du Livre, Fribourg, Switzerland

English translation published 1980
in the United States of America by:

Rizzoli INTERNATIONAL PUBLICATIONS, INC.
712 Fifth Ave.
New York, N.Y. 10019

All rights reserved
No parts of this book may be reproduced in any manner whatsoever without permission of Rizzoli International Publications, Inc.

Library of Congress Catalog Card number: 80-51168
ISBN: 0-8478-0322-8

Printed and bound in Switzerland

CONTENTS

Preface	7
I	
Dutch Faience before Production Began at Delft	9
Plates 1-6	11-16
II	
Materials and Manufacture	17
III	
Historical Setting: Trade Guilds, Masters, Trade Problems	19
IV	
Seventeenth and Early Eighteenth Centuries	21
Blue-and-white	21
'Mixed Technique'	23
The Work of Gÿsbrecht Claesz Verhaast	24
High-temperature Polychrome Painting	24
White Faience	24
Stonewares	25
Shapes	26
Plates 7-61	27-72
V	
The Rapid Rise in Production in the Early Eighteenth Century	73
High-temperature Decoration: European Designs	73
High-temperature Decoration: Far Eastern Style	74
Coloured Grounds	75
Delft *Doré*	75
Enamelling: Low-temperature Decoration Applied over the Glaze	76
Shapes	76
Plates 62-118	77-120
VI	
The Evolution of Styles and Shapes during the Eighteenth Century	121
Blue-and-white Ware	121
High-temperature Polychrome Painting	121
Factory Marks	121
The Influence of European Faience and Porcelain	122
Enamelled Ware	122
Shapes	122
Plates 119-48	124-49
VII	
'Peasant Delft'	150
Plates 149-54	151-4
VIII	
Figurines, Trompe-l'œil and Full Relief	155
Plates 155-68	157-69
IX	
Ornamental Plaques	170
Plates 169-73	171-5
X	
Dutch Tiles	176
Plates 174-6	177-8
XI	
Dutch Faience other than Delftware	180
Plates 177-9	180-1
XII	
The Role and Influence of Delftware in Europe	182
Conclusion	184
Plate 180	184-5
Factory Marks	187
Bibliography	195
Photo Credits	197
Index	198

TRANSLATOR'S NOTE

* The subject of this book is the pottery made at Delft in the seventeenth and eighteenth centuries, which is a tin-glazed earthenware. This term is unwieldy, and the less precise French word *faience*, now used frequently in English, is retained in this book.

For the faience manufactured at Delft, the editors of the English edition have preferred to adopt American usage and call it 'delftware', which in England is the old-fashioned term for post-Renaissance European tin-glazed earthenware, or 'faience' in general.

PREFACE

Delft spells faience,* even for those quite unversed in the history of ceramics. The city's reputation is universal.

It is rather surprising, therefore, that there was no study of faience from Delft for almost a century after production of the ware died out, until the appearance in 1878 of the book by Henry Havard. To write the history of Delft faience, Havard spent ten years among 'the principal collections of Europe... [assembling] ...those ceramic documents which should serve him as a starting point.' For five years more, he went through the archives in search of written documents so as to 'rejoin the repeatedly broken threads of this difficult study....' Havard thought his work definitive, and with whatever reservations, we have to admit that every authority depends on him. Havard quotes 47 collectors in different countries. This provides sufficient proof that oral knowledge, at least, of this admirable art of the Dutch potter has been of continuous interest to collectors since production ended at Delft. Although there was nothing written on the subject, it can confidently be asserted that collectors have always been interested in delftware.

All the great museums that contain ceramics have long preserved specimens of delftware, and from time to time the museums have been enriched by the acquisition of large and splendid collections, such as that of John Loudon, who lived at The Hague in the nineteenth century, which is now preserved in the Rijksmuseum, Amsterdam. No less fine, and perhaps larger, is that bequeathed by Albert Evenepoël to the Musées royaux d'Art et d'Histoire in Brussels. The Gemeente Museum at The Hague benefited from the admirable pieces collected by A.H.H. van der Burgh.

The famous Dutch faience centre of Delft was so renowned that, in England, the term 'delftware' began to be applied to all pottery that could be qualified as faience. The great English scholar Arthur Lane, writing in *Cahiers de la céramique et des arts du feu* (1957), gave his French readers the following explanation: 'delftware [is] the term used in England for [all] real faience, i.e. pottery with an (opaque) tin glaze....' As a result, Lane entitled his own article 'English delftware' to distinguish the faience he was discussing, which originated in England, from the Dutch wares. *

It appears that delftware was always appreciated in France also, for collectors such as Arosa, Cussac, Fétis, Gasnault, Guérard, Jourde, Liesville, Mandl, Montagne, Pannier, Pascal, Patrice Salin, Roullier and Sazerac de Forges made it possible for Havard to pursue his study. The Select Bibliography illustrates how knowledge of delftware gradually increased in spite of the great difficulties presented by the archives, which are abundant but often disappointing. Havard thought it worthwhile to publish a very long list of names found in the books of the trade guild. Attributions were made, some of which have had to be revised; every succeeding author has set out to try to put this whole question on a more secure footing.

It becomes clear that, except perhaps for the first period, it is generally pointless to attribute one or another type of delftware to a definite kiln; in fact, the head of a faience factory aimed at making and decorating his pieces in the fashion, following the taste of the day. Potters and painters certainly moved from factory to factory but continued working in the same style as before. This is known to have happened in other centres, Italy or France, for example. This is an important consideration to bear in mind throughout our examination of the beauties of delftware.

We have sought to provide guide-lines for understanding the contribution of the Dutch genius to the history of faience and have attempted to set such creativity in a historical framework, to re-emphasize the importance of the trade-guild spirit and describe the concern of Delft potters to bring delight and harmony to the domestic interiors of their contemporaries. Delftware is indeed a creation worthy to be included among the major phases of ceramic history.

We owe a deep debt of gratitude to all those whose knowledge and generosity have made possible the writing and illustration of this text. It seems right to express our obligation as much to the 'ancients', from whom we have gained so much information, as to those who have written recently on delftware. Thanks to Dutch, English, Belgian and French museums and to collectors (who prefer to remain anonymous), we hope that this near-complete survey of such a lovely product and its development will play its part in bringing others to enjoy what has been to us such a source of delight.

I DUTCH FAIENCE BEFORE PRODUCTION BEGAN AT DELFT

The origins of delftware lie rooted in the extraordinary history of pottery in the Netherlands and cannot be properly understood apart from the appearance of majolica in this part of Europe. The term 'majolica' (from the earlier name for Majorca) is in itself an indication of the sources of Western faience: Spain and Italy.

The historical context in which Dutch faience arose can only be cursorily mentioned here. As always, the history of pottery gives a faithful account of the phases of a country's development and civilization. A few facts from the troubled past of the industrious Netherlands will suffice to explain many turns of the story: after the death of Marie, daughter of Charles the Bold of Burgundy, the Netherlands became Austrian; in 1519 the Netherlands came under Spanish control through Charles V. The Reformation played a determining role in this region, causing an irreversible upheaval in Dutch history: the conflict between Catholic Spanish overlords and the Calvinist princes of Orange-Nassau. The struggle intensified until in 1648 the seven United Provinces—as the independent Netherlands were called—were recognized by the Treaty of Westphalia. This very simplified historical account shows how an art of Mediterranean origin could take root in this part of northern Europe.

In the beginning, it was Antwerp that benefited from knowledge of faience in the Italian manner. This was important enough for Cipriano Piccolpasso to have noted it in *Li Tre Libri dell'Arte del Vasaio (The Three Books of the Potter's Art)*, in which he wrote that Guido da Savino went to that city to practise the art of majolica early in the sixteenth century. The ceramic production of Antwerp lies outside the scope of this book, but it must be recognized as a crucial stage, which prepared the way for the appearance of faience in Holland. The fact that the names of many faience potters can be found in the United Provinces from the third quarter of the sixteenth century is often explained by their need to leave Antwerp for religious reasons. Several of them certainly bear names that were already known in Antwerp: Joris Andries left the guild of Antwerp in 1552 and settled at Middelburg in Zealand in 1564. He was perhaps the first faience potter established in the northern states. The faience potter of Haarlem, Adriaen Bogaert, has frequently been linked with Jan Bogaert of Antwerp. Another member of this family set up in Amsterdam; others founded workshops in Dordrecht.

In Haarlem we find one of the names that most intrigues ceramic historians: the adventurous Henrich Vroom, son of a potter. We are told by Carel van Mander, who wrote the *Livre des peintres (Book of Painters)* in 1604, that Vroom left his father's house as a painter and travelled throughout Europe following a strange itinerary consequent on the 'hazards of navigation'. (He is known to have painted marine pictures.) Vroom went from Eenkhuysen to Bruges, from Rotterdam to Spain, from Spain to Italy (notably to Florence, then to Rome to the painter Paul Bril). After a year in Venice, he went to Albissola and to Savona, passing through Milan and Genoa, then returned to Holland by way of Lyons and Rouen. Henrich Vroom died in Haarlem in 1640. All the authorities state that he continued to make faience as well as to paint, and that he often relied on his ceramic art to keep body and soul together. Ferrand Hudig even supposes that when he was in Seville Vroom was in touch with the famous Pisan, Francesco Niculoso. Vroom certainly did a lot of work in Venice, and Venetian influence is very clear in some of the early phases of Dutch faience.

Several categories can in fact be distinguished in what is called 'Dutch majolica'. If we try to pick out the different trends in this first faience production, immediately a Spanish element can be recognized, especially on tiles decorated with fruit: grapes and pomegranates, sometimes with the addition of floral motifs (usually tulips), are all treated in bold polychrome. The great period of such polychrome was throughout the first half of the seventeenth century, but its origins, in a rather more geometric guise, go back to the late sixteenth century. To this same geometric trend belongs a Frisian ware of the early seventeenth century, with multiple combinations of rosettes, stars, spirals and quartering, all in rather crude colours: blue, yellow, orange, green.

As well as these pieces in the Spanish style, Italian influence is manifest in a more precise manner. Potters either took their inspiration from figure scenes (which is perhaps the rarest), with occasional mythological or biblical subjects, or else followed the Raphaelesque tradition, with grotesques and putti comparable to those on Italian ware from Urbino to Deruta.

Three types of Dutch production can be set apart; they seem to be solely inspired by the genius of the Dutch potters themselves. The first type includes dishes with a central design: flowers or fruit, a figure or a religious inscription in Dutch. The rims are curiously treated with a raised frieze of fleurons; such friezes are peculiar to the Netherlands. The second type of production, though it has a blue ground in common with Venetian ware, is also very distinctive, with polychrome effects—not always felicitous—on its thick blue ground. A third type consists of a strange mixture of Italian and Chinese ideas. This is a quite extraordinary accomplishment: a background of blue designs in Chinese Transitional style from the end of the Ming dynasty, characterized by scenes at the water's edge including animals, deer in particular, or insects, sets off vivid orange medallions. (The range of colours is restricted.) Although traces of Mediterranean influence remain on a few of these pieces, it is here that the first real manifestation of the new Far Eastern contribution appears, that was to leave so strong a mark on Dutch wares. We shall see later the connection between the imports of porcelain and the interpretation made of different types by the Dutch potters. The founding of the Dutch East India Company in 1602 marks the beginning of the taste for blue-and-white decoration. Contrary to what has often been written, it was not invented at Delft but certainly preceded delftware, both for tile decoration and for vessels decorated completely in the new style.

The ways in which these different trends were combined were extremely varied. Blue-and-white decoration was the most popular. It required a quality of glaze able to compete with the appearance of porcelain. The style of decoration was always European, whether in the form of armorial devices, emblems or reflections of the predominant Dutch pictorial art then at its height, and attribution is thus difficult. It has not yet been possible, for example, to find a precise attribution for the ornamental plaques, such as the one in the Musées royaux d'Art et d'Histoire, Brussels, which depicts a lively kermess scene, with animation worthy of an engraver.

A typical case of difficult attribution is that of Claes Jansz Wÿtmans (or Wijtmans) of Rotterdam. Letters patent of 1614, granted by the States General, gave him the exclusive right to manufacture, or cause to be manufactured, every kind of object from the 'porcelain' of his invention for five years in the United Provinces. These objects, in both decoration and material, were almost comparable with the pieces imported from abroad. It has been inferred that here might be found the origin of a new kind of faience more closely resembling porcelain. F. Hudig quotes other individuals who were also ambitious to produce a new and better faience, particularly the potter Willem Jansz Verstraeten in Haarlem who, strangely, gave his son the benefit of his secret of 'manufacturing fine porcelain of Holland' while reserving his own right to continue manufacturing the old faience in the Italian and Spanish manner, called *straets goet* (Straits' goods), because they were shipped through the Straits of Gibraltar.

1   Dish: Dutch faience, high-temperature polychrome, *c.* 1620. D. 32.5 cm. Musée national de Céramique, Sèvres: inv. 22 675, Chompret Bequest.

The decoration of this dish is entirely in the Italian 'grotesque' style, derived from the designs made by the Urbino factory in the second half of the sixteenth century, based on paintings in the Loggia of the Vatican by Giovanni da Udine, a pupil of Raphael. The Umbrian factory of Deruta adopted this type of ornament, reproduced in a rougher manner. It is in this guise that the potters of the Netherlands took it as their model, and for this reason much care is needed in distinguishing the two rather similar wares. The palette is very simple, limited to blue, orange-yellow and manganese-brown. Our feeling is that the Dutch glaze is more unctuous than that used at Deruta.

The child leaning on a globe in the centre of the medallion is also directly borrowed from the Italian style. In some cases the grotesques may be in a single ring or, more rarely as here, arranged in two concentric zones, because of the size of the piece.

2   Dish: Dutch faience, high-temperature polychrome, early 17th century. D. 45 cm. Musée national de Céramique, Sèvres: inv. 22 412.

This dish belongs to a distinct type that still follows the traditions of majolica but already has a marked local character. The mythological subject occupying the centre of the dish is 'The Loves of Venus and Mercury'. This scene, and motifs in the cartouches surrounding it on the rim, are taken from engravings by Jean Muller, after Bartholomeus Spranger. This is a typical creation of the artists of the northern schools, who were strongly influenced by Italian art. A Latin inscription is partly visible round the cavetto: *Sine Fomite Frustra Fortior est delectat ma urit precibus Haud vinci Potest*.

3 Dish: Dutch faience, high-temperature polychrome, *c.* 1620. D. 34.5 cm. Musée national de Céramique, Sèvres: inv. 22 671, Chompret Bequest.

This dish shows two characteristics of one kind of early Dutch faience production. First, the decoration of the border with a blue ground and with raised knobs in relief — these were sometimes used on dishes to frame religious inscriptions and sometimes on fruit bowls. Second, the main design shows a Dutch officer on horseback, in every respect similar to the one on a dish discovered in the excavations at Rotterdam and preserved in the Boymans van Beuningen Museum there. The broadly sketched terrace closely resembles those found on certain tiles of the same period. The marks left by the three kiln supports on the front of the dish should also be noted: they are like those on Spanish dishes. Although the palette is limited to blue, green and orange-yellow and a touch of manganese-purple, the liveliness of these colours already creates a very rich impression. The back bears the inscription ELIAS.

3

4 Dish: Dutch faience, high-temperature polychrome, c. 1600. D. 32.5 cm. Musée national de Céramique, Sèvres: inv. 10 377.

The decoration of this dish is applied on a thick blue ground, in French often called *bleu d'empois,* 'starch blue'. Faience thus coloured was produced at several centres: in Italy at Faenza, then at Venice from the sixteenth century (where the blue ground is called *smaltino*), in France at Nevers from the mid-seventeenth century (where the ground is sometimes called *bleu persan,* 'Persian blue'). This type is often said to have been made to compete with Oriental pottery. Given the dates of its production, Dutch faience of this type must necessarily follow a Venetian influence rather than one from Nevers.

The Oriental character is reaffirmed by the running hare, so beloved of Persian art. Other motifs also occur, such as birds or even human figures. The designs are applied in opaque (barium) white on the blue ground, so as to isolate the supplementary colours.

5 Two-handled porringer: Dutch faience, high-temperature polychrome, early 17th century. D. 23 cm. Musée national de Céramique, Sèvres: inv. 9 012.

This type of ware, comprising bowls, dishes and porringers, has frequently been attributed to Antwerp. Discoveries made during excavations in Holland have shown, however, that it was more likely to have been made there. It represents a very important phase in the development of a Dutch style of ceramic decoration and combines two totally different sources of inspiration. The madonna in the centre, rendered in very simple polychrome, still reflects Italian influence. Sometimes there is a mythological subject in place of a religious figure. The framing decoration, however, reproduces Chinese motifs of the Transitional period at the end of the Ming dynasty. This may be considered the initial borrowing from that style made by Dutch potters, before they achieved their close imitations (see Pl. 32). The back of this piece is covered with a lead glaze. The handles, or ears, with lobed edges certainly go back to the origins of Dutch faience.

6 Plaque with indented edge: Dutch faience, blue-and-white, 18th century. L. 35 cm. Musée national de Céramique, Sèvres: inv. 9 679.

This interesting plaque has often been illustrated. Its Delft origin is not certain, and it is possible that it comes from another centre, such as Makkum. The picture of potters in action is nonetheless interesting. We see the throwers at work, the 'treader' working the clay, the enameller, the kiln and the pieces (not to scale) drying on shelves. The scene is depicted in a very simple style, probably the work of an apprentice.

II MATERIALS AND MANUFACTURE

Delftware has many peculiarities that distinguish it from other faience and help to identify it. One aspect is its weight, which is relatively light. Apart from pieces from Lille in France, and some faiences from Anspach in Germany, none has as light a body as delftware. This can be attributed to the Dutch concern to compete with the porcelain of the East India Company, which was so much admired in Holland.

Gerrit Paape tells us in his treatise *De Plateelbakker of Delftsch Aardewerk Maaker* (*The Faience Potter or Maker of Delft Clay Ware*), published in 1794, that to make what he—incorrectly—calls 'Delft porcelain', three kinds of clay are needed: black, *Rhijnlandsche*, clay from the Rhineland, clay from Tournai in Flanders and another found in the neighbourhood of Delft itself. The latter clay is light buff with quite a close grain. Gerrit Paape prescribes 'six ordinary barrow-loads of Tournai clay, three of Rhine clay, two of Delft....' The importance given to Tournai is clear. This excellent clay is in fact found at Bruyelles, a little village near Tournai. It was so much in demand that, when that part of the country was under French control, a royal edict of 1688 laid down 'from six to forty livres per load as the extraction rights on the derle or faience clay that foreigners, especially from Delft, came to collect'.

Henry Havard, who translated parts of Paape's work into French in 1878, describes the traditional preparation of the mixture: washing, weathering ('rotting') and kneading ('pugging'). Washing of the clays is known to have been done especially carefully at Delft, and this accounts for the exceptional fineness of the body. Gerrit Paape illustrates the system of basins that allowed a faultless selection of material. Havard describes the pugging with some amusement: 'an operation best done with bare feet, because one can thus discover the hard lumps and crush them or separate them from the heap....' After this preparation, the clay is divided up into balls, each of which is kneaded again before being brought to the thrower. The craftsman-thrower (*de draaier*) shapes his piece on the usual potter's wheel, before giving it its first ('biscuit') firing. Then the glazer or *greever* dips it in a bath of white (*wit*) consisting of 50 pounds of tin ash (oxide), 56 pounds of mastic, a half pound of smalt (blue ground) and 5.5 ounces of copper filings. It is then held in a vertical position for a short time before being put to dry on a plank covered with nails driven in half way. It seems likely that this is how the glaze on the backs of Delft plates and dishes acquired all those characteristic little holes.

After the preparation, the pieces are decorated, using stencils or pricked drawings, and the transparent lead glaze or *kwaart* is applied, which is so characteristic of Dutch faience and is comparable to the Italian *coperta*. Gerrit Paape gives us the recipe: 36 pounds of mastic (a mixture of sand, salt and soda), 42 pounds of litharge of gold (i.e. oxide of lead), 4 pounds of potash, 7 pounds of salt. This glaze is sprinkled on and brushed; it has a special, brilliant, glassy sheen designed to emulate the gloss of porcelain. The characteristic outlining of designs on some delftware is obtained by the use of *trek*, a dark colour ranging from black to bluish purple. With it the decorator emphasized the contours of his designs.

The palette of delftware consists of blue (from cobalt), purple or brown (from manganese), yellow (from antimony), red (from iron) and green (from copper). These are basically the colours that can resist a high-temperature firing.

Gerrit Paape quotes two formulae for yellow: '9 pounds of antimony, 7 pounds of litharge of gold, 1.5 pounds of salt.... This mixture is divided into small parts that are placed on rough clay plates and baked. However, to prevent the mixture from adhering to the plates, care is taken to rub them with sand and place them at the top of the kiln....' The second means of obtaining yellow consists of '10 pounds of antimony, 6 pounds of litharge of gold, 2 pounds of oxide of lead, 3 pounds of salt...by placing this mixture on little plates and baking it twice or thrice, a good yellow is obtained....'

Red was always a problem for makers of high-temperature faience, because the metal oxides that produce this colour are unstable at the temperature at which the piece is fired. Dutch potters, therefore, adopted the method already used in the Near East and in Italy, which consisted of applying a red slip (that is, red ochre, called 'Armenian bol' in Italian majolica). Gerrit Paape notes: 'good bolus [Armenian bol] burnt five or six times, taking care to stir it during firing, gives quite a good red....' Gerrit Paape's treatise dates from 1794, a very decadent period for the art of pottery-making, and he only speaks of high-temperature or *grand-feu* production, thereby omitting a large proportion of the many inventions which make Delft pottery outstanding, the history of which we have to trace.

Depending on the period or the artist, three different methods of fixing decoration by firing were used at Delft. First and foremost was painting under or in the glaze in high-temperature *(grand-feu)* colours; second was 'mixed technique' and finally enamelling *(petit feu)*. In the first method, the pieces are packed in the clay boxes called saggars (usually cylindrical) that are supported by pegs projecting from the sides; they are then placed in a very simple kiln. The firing temperature reaches about 750° or 800° Centigrade. When they come out, the pieces are finished and ready to sell.

The 'mixed technique' brought an added richness to the palette of the Delft ceramic painters from the late seventeenth century onwards. The use of a flux—an alkaline or metallic element used to promote the fusion of a glaze—allowed additional colours to be applied after the first firing: a piece was first decorated in blue, or blue and green, and fired. Subsequently the painter added low-temperature *(petit feu)* enamel colours: red from gold (called purple of Cassius), gold and sometimes other colours. This decoration was submitted to a much cooler firing in a muffle kiln. The process was, of course, much more costly than a single high firing, which is no doubt why it had disappeared by Paape's day.

The origins of overglaze enamelling go back to the thirteenth century, and to appreciate it, we must review the different stages in the appearance of that technique. In *Poteries et porcelaines chinoises (Chinese Pottery and Porcelain)*, Daisy Lion-Goldschmidt writes, 'The first enamels appear towards the end of the Song period with reds and greens of [Japanese] *aka-e* type.' In the same period there was similar activity in Seljuk Iran with *mina'i* wares, overglaze-painted Islamic pottery. Glass painters (both Venetian and German) also used fluxes for applying designs on glass. Lastly there was the work of the painter on glass *(Hausmaler)*. From about 1660, painters on glass, most of them German, lighted on the idea of adding decoration to white faience and Chinese porcelains. At Delft, too, during the seventeenth century, certain painters decorated pieces imported from China, Japan and Saxony. Having discovered the use of fluxes, some faience potters went on to decorate pieces entirely with enamel colours.

Another activity highly characteristic of the Delft potters should not be forgotten: red stoneware. This cannot be called faience, for it is a very fine sandy clay intended primarily to imitate Yixing stoneware. Since the sixteenth century, Yixing had been an important Chinese centre for stoneware; it specialized in red stoneware teapots with relief or engraved decoration. The manufacture of red stoneware played a very important role at Delft: the material was used mainly to make teapots to compete with those imported from the Far East.

Pls. 52-3

Having surveyed the techniques of Dutch potters, we can now review the characteristics that identify delftware. The fine body and light weight has already been mentioned, also the sheen, applied to the surface with the transparent lead glaze or *kwaart*. The glazes themselves were rigorously chosen and handled. There are, as well, the numerous little holes frequently found on the backs of plates or on the bases of vases. When considering style, it is important to bear in mind the main aim that obsessed Dutch potters: to emulate Chinese porcelain. On this subject, Isaac Lelong, a historiographer of Delft, wrote in his *Kabinet van Nederlandsche en Kleessche Outheden (Collection of Netherlandish Antiques)* (Amsterdam, 1732): 'here the main industry within Delft is the pottery or porcellanery [porcelain-works] whose products, both to distinguish them from the wares of the Orient and because they are superior to all the others manufactured elsewhere in the country, are called "Delft porcelains"....' This is an indispensable factor to consider when studying delftware, but it should be stressed that none of these characteristics can be used as a criterion by itself.

III HISTORICAL SETTING: TRADE GUILDS, MASTERS, TRADE PROBLEMS

It is still something of a mystery why the city of Delft became one of the chief centres of faience production. First, we must seek the historical reasons and place ourselves in a mid-seventeenth-century context. After the Treaty of Westphalia in 1648, Jan de Witt assumed power as Grand Pensionary of the Netherlands. This was the beginning of a seventeen-year struggle against England, arising out of the first English Navigation Acts. The Triple Alliance with England and Sweden, established by the Treaty of Aix-la-Chapelle, dates from 1668. A new page in the history of the Netherlands was begun by the invasion of that country by the armies of the French king, Louis XIV, in 1672. Holland opened her dykes to the sea. William III, the son born posthumously to William II of Nassau, arrived to become chief of state (*stathouder*) in Holland and then, in 1688, king of England. The political events that eliminated the chief of state's privy council (*stathouderat*) and resurrected it once again with the Peace of Utrecht in 1713, subjected the Netherlands to prosperity and regression alternately, the importance of which it is not easy to calculate.

These few glimpses show how the country at that time was obliged to identify its interests successively with those of various other European countries. The traditions of the northern lands had the strongest influence on Dutch customs. The essentially maritime character of Dutch trade dictated that its main contacts were through the great commercial ports: the sensitive spots in this land, vulnerable to invasion from every direction. The ports are perhaps one of the reasons why potters chose to settle in Delft, for this locality has no one obvious advantage. The majority of potting families certainly were not native to the region. The economic problems caused by the increasing decline of Delft's breweries since the early seventeenth century are always mentioned, as are the city's great ordeals: the fire of 1536, the destruction of 1608, the explosion of the powder magazine in 1654. It would seem, however, that one important industry still thrived in Delft: cloth.

Amidst the grandeurs and miseries of that city, the corporate spirit was more than usually stimulated by the need for defence and mutual help. Henry Havard sought to recover the whole history of delftware through the archives of the Guild of Saint Luke, which included painters, potters, sculptors, scabbard-makers, printers and print and picture dealers. Under the title *La Gilde de Saint Luc*, Havard attempted a complete account of the organization that, because it appeared later than at Haarlem or Amsterdam, rose to incomparable power in an astonishingly short time. The official foundation of the guild goes back to 29 May 1611, and the character, development and even the spirit of delftware can only be understood in the context of the rigorous conditions under which the craft of master faience potter or *plateelbakker* (literally 'dishmaker', to distinguish it from the 'tilemaker' whose products were not considered as choice) was instituted.

Crafts were closely protected but very strictly supervized by the syndics. When the tax farmers attempted, on several occasions, to impose dues on the raw materials, the burgomasters stood up to them, thanks to the guilds. What we would now call social security was set up quite early, with sickness funds and old-age pensions for members.

Recruitment into the potters' guild was organized according to fixed rules: an apprentice had to have worked for six years under three masters who were members of the guild—two years in each workshop. After that he was invited to show proof of his ability before a jury of master potters. The regulations of 20 April 1654 decreed that a thrower had to make a ewer, a salad bowl and a salt-cellar with a hollow stem, 'thrown from one piece of clay'. A painter had to decorate six dishes of the largest size and entirely cover a fruit bowl with designs; then he had to throw or paint a pile of 30 plates. Once received into the guild, the candidate had to pay his mastery dues, and Havard explains how the entry of these dues in the books of the guild gives us valuable information about the individuals concerned. The number of masters is surprising, but very often it is difficult to identify their work. Famous marks are often disappointing in the information they can provide. Though the workshops of the late seventeenth and early eighteenth centuries are easily recognized, soon afterwards the letters and signs refer more to factories than to the work of an artist.

The masters were a 'watch-dog' committee within the guild, as shown by the famous order of 1764, which obliged the '*plateelbakkers* to register a pertinent and precise memorandum containing a description of their factory sign with the mark they are accustomed to put on their pieces.' It is worth remembering that measures had to be taken during that period against the counterfeiting of marks, which must have become quite frequent.

Another activity of the guild masters was the organization of protective measures; they even went so far as to envisage a trade treaty with America and the prohibition of foreign faiences. There is no reference, of course, to imports of porcelain from the Far East.

The role Holland played in importing Far Eastern ceramics must be emphasized and several points considered. Commercial activity had intensified since Holland supplanted Portugal in long-distance sea voyages. The Dutch East India Company plied the seas. Daisy Lion-Goldschmidt recounts in *Poteries et porcelaines chinoises* how large cargoes of Far Eastern products began arriving in Amsterdam early in the seventeenth century. Holland gave certain of these wares the name *kraak-porselein*, a term that evokes the picturesque beginnings of this trade's history in alluding to certain cargoes of *caraque*-type ships seized by the Dutch fleet from the Portuguese; *kraak-porselein* became the name even for imitations made in Holland. Pl. 71

Following certain political developments in China and the less than brilliant circumstances of the Dutch East India Company towards the end of the seventeenth century, Holland turned to Japan for trade, though she still maintained some contact with regions of China remote from the great porcelain factory of Jingdezhen. The Dutch managed to establish a privileged position for themselves in Japan, so that many pieces inspired by the Far East were no longer representative of Chinese tastes, but of Japanese.

IV SEVENTEENTH AND EARLY EIGHTEENTH CENTURIES

BLUE-AND-WHITE

Early seventeenth-century delftware, as we explained in Chapter II, is not easy to identify. Some pieces have been considered by certain writers as the incunabula of this art: the famous kermess ornamental plaque (1640) in the Musées royaux d'Art et d'Histoire, Brussels, and the dish with the Battle of Vught (1634 and marked C.H.) preserved in the same museum. Attributions of these pieces to one or another potter of Delft have no precise foundation.

Many writers, from Ferrand Hudig onwards, understandably have reservations about the attribution of the kermess plaque. This amazing scene, in the manner of Jacobis Jordaens, treated in a rather unusual blue, has a series of commentaries devoted to it, none of them conclusive. It is worth citing the opinion of Hudig, author of *Delfter Fayence*, who disputed Havard's theory that pieces overcrowded with figures in this way are characteristic of early delftware. Many other tiles or panels that no one has ever thought of attributing to Delft have the same style of decoration and colouring and are of the same period.

The ornamentation of the Battle of Vught dish, in our opinion, reflects the persistence of traditional decoration. The frieze of putti and little flowers on the rim is still very Italian; the design is in blue-and-white, but there is still something reminiscent of Castelli faience in it. The monogram, C.H., has frequently been attributed to Cornelis H. Valckenhoff, said to be the first faience potter established at Delft, but J. Helbig has very pertinently questioned this, observing that 'it could equally well be attributed to Cornelis Huybrechtsz, a Delft faience potter mentioned in 1617, or to some other Dutch potter of the second quarter of the seventeenth century....'

The situation changes in the second half of the seventeenth century, when the styles of the great masters crystallized and their characteristics became distinguishable. We will begin with three of them: Frederik van Frÿtom (also known as van Frijtom), Samuel van Eenhoorn and Adriaen Kocks, who are particularly prominent in their handling of blue-and-white. But first, an exceptional piece in the Rijksmuseum, dated 1670, should be mentioned. It was based on contemporary engravings, and its decoration is reminiscent of the lively kermess scene on the ornamental plaque in the Musées royaux d'Art et d'Histoire, Brussels.

The work of Frederik van Frÿtom has recently been studied by A. Vecht. This writer has attempted a corpus of the masterly work of this painter who made the faience technique his medium. Strangely enough, there is no reference to Van Frÿtom in the guild registers. His name has been found, however, in a number of legal documents. He must have been born about 1632; in 1652, he married in Delft. He is thought to have been a good family man; he attended the Calvinist church, where he met many artists, and he is even said to have maintained relations with great contemporary painters. Van Frÿtom made his will in 1695 and died in 1702.

It is interesting that Van Frÿtom worked in the factory of Lambertus Cleffius: F. Hudig and E. Neurdenburg thought this probable, and A. Vecht has confirmed it by the discovery of two plaques with the mark C.L. interlaced. There is no doubt that the work of Frederik van Frÿtom is outstanding in the history of delftware. It consists of three categories: rectangular or octagonal plaques and panels, with landscapes or church interiors, often dated around 1660; dishes with the same kind of decoration in the centre; lastly jugs, ewers and even some cruets. While Van Frÿtom's style is wholly European, Samuel van Eenhoorn, whose frequent signature is well known, created works of Far Eastern inspiration. Van Eenhoorn was one of the most important people in the Greek A factory, which belonged to his father Wouter van Eenhoorn. The period during which Samuel was the owner was quite short; he received it as a wedding gift in 1678, and he died in 1686. But he is already mentioned in the factory as shareholder (*winkelhouder*) as early as 1674. The signature S.V.E. was thus probably used between 1674 and 1686. It can also be assumed that the mark was employed by Samuel's heirs for a time after his death.

Pl. 16 Other contemporary factories, less easily identified, certainly worked in the same Far Eastern style. All the same, we may consider that the characteristic interpretation of Kangxi blue-and-white decoration began with the factory of Samuel van Eenhoorn. During the Kangxi period (1662-1722), Chinese blue-and-white ware was of a very high quality. The Chinese decoration, applied all over or in rectangular frames, consisted of varied motifs, in particular floral ones, or of landscapes, some of which included figures. There is indisputably a 'Samuel van Eenhoorn style' based on these wares. Its distinctive traits include: a bluish tinge in the glaze (the blue often heightened with manganese-purple to a special intensity), many Chinese-type scenes and decorative motifs evidently borrowed from the Oriental repertoire, such as friezes of floral scrolls or tulip stems placed on bottle Pl. 17 necks. The shapes, too, are varied, and some are rather strange. There are several spice boxes with vertical partitions and curiously contorted shapes bearing the signa-Pl. 15 ture S.V.E. His mark is also on the famous spouted gourd in the Musées royaux d'Art et d'Histoire, Brussels, which is an exact replica of a Chinese form.

The third great master, Adriaen Kocks, is also connected with the Greek A factory. He married Judith van Eenhoorn and was director of that factory from 1687 until his death in 1701. The very fine series of faiences with the monogram A.K. has given rise to much confusion in the past, but Arthur Lane, in *A Guide to Tiles*, clarified the problem with his discovery proving incontrovertibly that all pieces marked A.K. could be distinguished as the work of Adriaen Kocks. While working on the monumental vases at Hampton Court that bear this mark, Lane found the order from William III of Orange, who had become king of England, to the master Pls. 26-8 of the Greek A factory.

The production of Adriaen Kocks is always of high quality. It includes, in addition to the monumental pieces Pls. 18-21 already referred to, a great variety of shapes: flower vases, lidded jars, barber's bowls, vases for sets, bowls, tea caddies, plates (sometimes with very elaborate outlines), as well as the large conical cream pans with a flat bottom, some of which are decorated with special care.

While the Far Eastern style is almost always evident, Kocks sometimes combines it in a strange manner with elements inherited from European designers. These elements are particularly visible on the large pieces that show the influence of Daniel Marot, architect, decorator, engraver and designer.

Marot, son of a Parisian architect, used the designs of the famous Bérain brothers as his models. He was among the Protestant Huguenot artists who were forced to leave France at the revocation of the Edict of Nantes (22 October 1685). Marot found a welcome in the Netherlands, where he began work for the *Stathouder* William III of Orange. Roger Weigert has shown how Daniel Marot Pls. 22-24 gradually abandoned his purely French style and adapted to local tastes. He also notes how Marot's development did not keep pace with ideas current in France during the Pl. 25 same period. His engravings were the source of many new forms and ornamental compositions on faience plaques. Marot's interest in ceramics is shown by the prominence given to it in his decorative compositions. For example, in what he called a 'French-style room', there were a considerable number of vases, distributed from floor to ceiling on consoles and cornices.

Although some of the work of Adriaen Kocks reflects Marot's influence, much more is of Chinese inspiration. Pls. 19, 21 Kocks had a rare felicity in his interpretations of Kangxi style, producing at times delightfully fantastic scenes. His decoration includes the lacy lambrequin motifs, scallops that were to be popular in Delft for many years. They have a double origin, for they they were used in China, but the Dutch significantly named them 'French stitch' (*fransche Punt*). Pls. 18, 51

Adriaen Kocks often made use of the dark-coloured outlines called *trek*. It has been observed that Kocks's monogram is often followed by a number. It must be remembered however, as C.H. de Jonge has pointed out, that there is a possibility that the mark A.K. was used by another individual who held the important position of dean of the guild in the mid-seventeenth century: Aelbrecht Cornelisz Keyser, who was active between 1635 and 1667 in the Two Boats factory. Keyser might be the author of a few pieces of blue-and-white in an earlier style than Kocks, which reflected the Chinese Wanli style. Wares of the Wanli period (1573-1620) in China were blue-and-white and characterized by genre scenes based on legends, by landscapes or by furnishings.

'Fishbone'-shaped plants, banana leaves and the traditional Chinese 'clouds' were particularly notable motifs on such Chinese wares. Keyser then would be the artist responsible for making 'Wanli-style' decoration develop towards 'Kangxi style'. There are also 'mixed technique' faiences with the A.K. mark (in some cases even made for the same destination as the blue-and-white pieces), for instance, examples made for Hampton Court.

Pl. 26
Pls. 27-8

Blue-and-white ware of the late seventeenth century is not confined to the work of the three potters mentioned here. While attributions to these masters are quite well established, there are many contemporary products; some have distinguishing marks and come from known factories; others are anonymous but are manifestly of the same period and inspiration. Some names of other great makers of blue-and-white are known in the late seventeenth century. We have already spoken of Lambertus Cleffius when discussing Frederik van Frÿtom. He was the son of the owner of several faience factories at Delft, a man of some substance. Nothing is known of the factories' wares, but Lambertus in his Metal Pot factory was (until his death in 1691) one of the leading figures in the guild. Like his father, he took out shares in other factories, then resold them. His production has often been compared with that of Samuel van Eenhoorn: the same shapes, the same style and often the same dark-coloured outlines (*trek*).

Pl. 32
Pls. 29-31

Another important figure is Gerrit Pietersz Kam. In his case, confusion is rife and questions insoluble. As J. Helbig observes, the initials G.K. are not only those of both father and son (who had the same first names) but of another faience potter of some distinction: Gÿsbrecht (or Gijsbrecht) Lambrechtsz Kruyck. The first two began at the sign of the Three Golden Ash Barrels, then in 1701 they bought the Peacock factory. The Far Eastern type of design with large lambrequins and a rosette was one of the principal themes of the Kams' factory. Kruyck was a master in six different factories.

There is similar confusion over the two Van der Laans, both of whom always used the mark I.V.L. Attempts have been made to distinguish the work of father and son by style. All these factories also produced polychrome ware.

Pl. 152

Alongside these faiences marked with a monogram are pieces of the same period that are unmarked. Among them are all the types we have already studied. There are, for instance, a certain number of plaques or plates close to the style of Van Frÿtom, inspired by the engravings of the period, and even by portraits such as those of Protestant pastors that reflect the prints of Van Queborn. Other pieces are more or less Far Eastern in character. Whether or not a piece is monogrammed bears no relation to its artistic merit, as examination of these pieces very quickly proves.

Pl. 33

Pls. 34-5

'MIXED TECHNIQUE'

It was obviously out of this marvellous blossoming of blue-and-white faience that a new technique was born, one that constituted an event of prime importance in the history of Western ceramics. We have mentioned the appearance of what is called 'mixed technique', which consisted basically of applying to a piece already decorated in blue-and-white and fired, low-temperature (*petit feu*) colours and gilding fixed by a second low-temperature (muffle) firing. Such an innovation shows great skill in the technique of faience potting.

Pl. 37

Pl. 38

The practitioners in question are, on the one hand, the Hoppesteyns and, on the other, Adriaen Kocks. The Hoppesteyns should already have been mentioned, as they were among the makers of high-temperature blue-and-white faience of the late seventeenth century. Jacob Wemmersz Hoppesteyn owned faience factories at Delft from 1657: at the sign of the Axe factory, then at the Young Moor's Head factory, where he became co-proprietor with Jan Groelant. Jacob died in 1671, and his son Rochus Jacobsz succeeded him. Around 1690, the son established himself at the Old Moor's Head factory and died in 1692. It can safely be said that every piece bearing the mark of these two artists should be placed among the treasures of delftware. The famous mark, I.W., is on many pieces with a type of decoration that occurs later than the dates corresponding to the lives of Jacob Wemmersz and his son Rochus Jacobsz. Hence all authorities agree that a potter (probably the heir of the Hoppesteyns) still used this mark in the early eighteenth century.

Pls. 38-9

Pl. 40

Pls. 41-2

Pl. 43

The Hoppesteyns displayed a certain connection between their source of inspiration and their choice of technique. More than any other potters, perhaps, the Hoppesteyns placed mythological and biblical subjects, often borrowed from Italian iconography, in surroundings of Far Eastern inspiration. They drew their subjects from Raphael and equally from Giulio Romano

Pls. 38-40

or Polidoro da Caravaggio, and their mythological figures from the work of Tempesta (which they knew through the engravings of Giovanni-Battista Galestruzzi). They took ideas from Pietro Santo Bartoli and even from such Dutch engravers as Simon Frisius.

The frames on Hoppesteyn works show astonishing combinations of scrolls, interlace and floral motifs in robust polychrome: red, yellow, green and gold, strongly reminiscent of painted glass. The connection between the work of the Hoppesteyns and that of glass painters is obvious. As is to be expected, the influence of painting on glass (*Hausmalerei*) of more or less the same period should be borne in mind as well.

Pl. 45 The 'mixed technique' was adopted in the workshop of Adriaen Kocks, and a number of very fine pieces of this type, marked A.K., are known. Contrary to what is some-
Pl. 44 times thought, 'mixed technique' faiences with the A.K. mark are often quite equal in quality to those by the Hoppesteyns, though more locally inspired. In particular, there are motifs influenced by Daniel Marot. Presently, we shall see how the technique of Delft *doré* really provides the sequel to the 'mixed technique'.

THE WORK OF GŸSBRECHT CLAESZ VERHAAST

Another very special aspect of the inventive genius of the Dutch potter is represented by the still very enigmatic work of Gÿsbrecht (or Gijsbrecht) Claesz Verhaast. It is known that he worked about 1689 as a 'master dish-
Pl. 47 maker' (*meester plateelbakker*) at the Young Moor's Head factory and, therefore, must have been there with Rochus Jacobsz Hoppesteyn. Helbig recounts how Verhaast was often absent from the factory to work on his own, exploiting his knowledge of the handling of fluxes. This, no doubt, is what enabled him to execute his extraordinary little pictures of interiors or landscapes. There are very few: nine as far as we know. The mixture and application of colours are done in imitation oil painting, and the effect is very strange. Hudig comments on
Pl. 46 how difficult it is to tell whether the colours are in or over the glaze. The palette is blue, purple, grey, yellow, brown and pink. As Hudig says, these colours, placed side by side, show no sign of running or burning, such as would be inevitable with high-temperature firing. Hudig's conclusion seems excessively severe, that these pieces are 'ceramic curiosities of doubtful artistic value'.

HIGH-TEMPERATURE POLYCHROME PAINTING

High-temperature (*grand-feu*) polychrome painting was to take on great importance, but there is one problem that, in our opinion, has not yet been solved: its dating. We have seen that Dutch faience potters were familiar with high-temperature glazes by the late sixteenth and early seventeenth century, but when did they first appear at Delft? Almost every authority treats the lovely floral compositions directly inspired by flower painters as the first examples of Delft polychromes. De Jonge also Pl. 49 shares this opinion and in *Delft Ceramics* shows us an oval plaque decorated in the centre with a vase of roses and tulips: this type of faience she dates to around 1675. This means a gap of 25 to 30 years between the practice of polychrome decoration in the Dutch majolica tradition and its appearance at Delft. Several of these plaques are known, and it is rather surprising to find a technique of such high quality from the start. The appearance of several types of polychrome decoration can be dated to about the last decade of the seventeenth century. Following the descriptions used for Chinese pottery, these polychromes can be classed as 'three-colour ware' and 'five-colour ware'.

The timid polychromy of the 'three-colour ware' generally consists of blue, green and yellow, to represent, for Pl. 51 example, birds fluttering above a spray of flowers. It is often not easy to date this very simple type. When the number of colours increased to five, the great developments of the early eighteenth century began. This rich colour range allowed the creation of many celebrated designs, but the dates of their beginnings are much disputed. We shall, therefore, study them in the following chapter.

WHITE FAIENCE

Two more types of seventeenth-century delftware remain, which are often neglected. The first is white faience. The admiration in which Chinese white wares Pl. 50 called *blanc de Chine* were held in Europe is well known. They were in great demand, and pieces were mounted in bronze or silver. The Delft potter took up the challenge Pl. 48 and set about making bowls, ewers, bottles, even animals in imitation of the Chinese. It is impossible to see in photographs what extraordinary means were used to compete with the Chinese models. At the same time, from about the beginning of 1665, according to the inventories quoted by De Jonge, a more typically Dutch shape was produced: the handled jug called *kannetje*, with a pewter lid and a plain or fluted body. This type of vase is all the more interesting in that it figures in so many still-lifes and interiors painted at the time. In the eighteenth century, as we shall see, white faience was used for other purposes.

STONEWARES

The second type of pottery we cannot leave without a mention, even though it is not faience, is the famous red stoneware that Delft produced in the late seventeenth century. That ware was inspired by the Chinese teapots from Yixing, which arrived with the tea cargoes and of which the Dutch were probably the first importers. It is a fine reddish-brown ware with a mat surface. Demand for the pots increased as the popularity of the new drink grew, and Delft seems to have been among the first centres to imitate these Far Eastern stonewares. Several manufacturers' names are quoted; attributions are easy because most pieces bear a mark in relief, probably made with a seal. The best known marks are those of Ary-Jansz de Milde and of Jacobus de Caluwe. An amusing detail is often noted by writers on the subject: Ary de Milde, on registering his mark, is mentionned as 'Mr Theepotbacker' (teapot maker). [Pls. 52-3]

The shapes of this stoneware are very carefully formed: the body is globular, the spout conical, and there is a large handle, easy to hold. The decoration is generally a motif of flowering branches, done in relief, of course.

Was anything other than teapots made in this ware? It is true that there is mention of an octagonal bowl in the Gemeente Museum, Arnhem, but even it has a crowned teapot in relief in the centre.

SHAPES

It may surprise the reader to see how quickly Delft asserted its originality in the variety of shapes. The Dutch potter began with dishes and plates that had a sinuous, scalloped profile and flanged rim close to the Italian Renaissance type. But a simplification soon emerged. About 1680, a form of dish existed without a rim and very thin, resembling a skull-cap: these are called *pannekoekjes* (from *pannekook*, meaning pancake). [Pl. 106]

Tea brought a number of entirely Far Eastern forms: the globular teapot with flat facets or eight sides. With it, the rectangular or square tea caddy seems often to have been treated with great care; its circular neck generally had a very flat lid. It is odd that very few cups have been preserved. It is likely that most of them—strongly influenced by the Far East—were little handleless bowls with lobed sides, with saucers. Tureens seem to have been very rare at this early period. Examples of tableware appearing quite early are, not unexpectedly, spice jars with two handles and a lid, divided into compartments inside; jugs; ewers and the very special *rijsttafelstel*, which is a set of asymmetrical dishes that fit side by side round a central dish and are often termed sweetmeat dishes in English. This ensemble was designed for serving rice with its garnishes (*rijsttafel*). Concerning a similar set of dishes used in China, Daisy Lion-Goldschmidt writes in *Poteries et porcelaines chinoises*: 'for table use for dessert are the sweetmeat dishes, a series of small irregular dishes that fit together, often into the form of a lotus flower....' One of the first examples of this type is signed by the Hoppesteyns. Parts are in the Rijksmuseum and the Musée national de Céramique, Sèvres. [Pls. 52-3, 78, 99] [Pls. 17, 45, 92-3] [Pls. 32, 50] [Pl. 15] [Pls. 37, 39, 63, 105, 126] [Pl. 57] [Pls. 41-3]

Vases for holding flowers were an early stimulus to the potter's imagination, and what are called 'tulip vases' may sometimes appear to us as very bizarre constructions: they certainly gave scope for great virtuosity. These vessels, as documents of the time clearly show, were used for arranging not only tulips but also different varieties of flowers popular at the time. In size and shape they allowed of a degree of experiment that is sometimes disconcerting. The two best known shapes of tulip vases are the obelisk and the fan. The classic obelisk is composed of a square base on a foot with a series of square boxes rising above it. The base often rests on four figures. In some cases, the structure reached nearly two metres in height. [Pls. 54-5] [Pls. 18, 27-8, 54-5]

In an article in *Country Life* (January 1976), Michael Archer describes such extravagant constructions made for the Duke of Devonshire. One piece has a base resting on five legs surmounted by Negro heads on which are placed sphinxes. The upper part, for holding flowers, consists of five storeys of pagodas. These, like the obelisks of Hampton Court, are the work of Adriaen Kocks. The pyramids made for the royal palace are also quite original compositions, as the illustrations show. A more simple type of vase is produced by piling a series of globular vessels one above the other. This type was imitated in other places, notably at Savona in northern Italy. Obelisk tulip vases, as the great collector Van Gelder observed, have an Italian origin: the designer Daniel Marot knew the engravings of Sebastiano Serlio, after Vitruvius; Giuseppe Liverani showed two obelisks 71 centimetres high in majolica.

There are many other kinds of tulip vase. The fantasy of the Delft potter in this field seems to have been limitless. In the 'baluster' type vases, the lids are usually pierced with holes to hold the flower stems. Pl. 26

The fan-shaped tulip vase is more frequent. It consists of a footed vase; the body is flattened and heart-shaped or round, surmounted by a number of mouths arranged in a fan. These vases are often flanked by figures of winged dragons or, more rarely, human-headed monsters. Pls. 18, 103

Large, footed basins with extraordinary handles in the form of chimeras are in the same ornamental style. There are also rectangular boxes with holes in the top, for growing bulbs or holding cut flowers.

A collection of five or seven vases is a notion that originated with the 'garniture' set, made in the Far East and frequently exported during the Ming period (1368-1644). Such sets are called *de Kastels*, from *kast* (cupboard) and *stel* (set). This aptly describes the decorative intention of these vases, which were placed along the ledges of imposing cupboards in Dutch houses. A set consists of differently shaped vases, similarly treated. These include a lidded vase, christened potiche in the nineteenth century; the lid is generally dome shaped, with a very elaborate or a plain round knob. Alternating with these potiches (generally three in number) are beaker-shaped vases and bottles. Beakers may be round or octagonal. Bottles are pear shaped or faceted; alternatively the upper part of the bottle is waisted to make a double gourd. The mouths of these bottles are quite often flared. It is difficult to date the first appearance of a truncated pyramidal base on these bottles. It certainly became more frequent during the eighteenth century but already existed in the seventeenth. Pls. 56, 58 Pls. 29, 30, 36, 38, 73, 77, 91, 94, 101 113 Pls. 56, 58, 87 Pls. 16, 31, 79, 83, 103

Rarer as part of garniture sets are the cylindrical or *rouleau* vases. An additional number of shapes can be cited: openwork baskets and hemispherical vases of rather curious aspect, with two handles and a spout, which rested on three feet. Helbig writes in his catalogue: 'This type of pot resting on three small feet and provided with two handles was current in the Netherlands in the sixteenth and seventeenth centuries. There is one, for example, depicted in a print representing Autumn, engraved by Cock.... In this scene, the vessel serves to collect the blood of a butchered pig, but it could be used for many other purposes....' Other objects such as brush handles, wig stands and candlesticks appear at this time. Pl. 59 Pl. 60 Pl. 61

While these latter shapes are entirely European, the same cannot be said of a strange vessel that is an exact copy of a Ming piece. This is a 'drinking vessel' of gourd shape with a spout. There is one example signed Samuel van Eenhoorn preserved in the Musées royaux d'Art et d'Histoire, Brussels.

7

7 Dish: early delftware (?), blue-and-white, mark C.H., dated 1634. D. 44 cm. Musées royaux d'Art et d'Histoire, Brussels: inv. 236, Evenepoël Collection.

This dish was made famous by Henry Havard and has been discussed at length since. The date, 1634, would make it a pioneer piece of delftware, if the attribution to Delft were accepted as correct. The decoration in blue represents a battle scene, framed round the rim with a frieze of cupids and little flowers, all still in a very Italianate style. One can recognize some relationship with the style of Castelli faience. The subject is the Battle of Vught near Bois-le-Duc, which occurred, as Jean Helbig reminds us, 'on 5 February 1600 between nineteen Belgian cuirassiers led by Gérard Abrahams, called the *Kherbeetje,* whom we see in the foreground, and nineteen French cavalrymen commanded by the Sire de Bréauté in the pay of the United Provinces....' The same writer lists several possible translations of the monogram, C.H., that accompanies the date and observes that a Dutch theme already occupies the place of the usual Italian motifs.

8 Rectangular plaque: Dutch faience, blue-and-white, dated 1640. H. 58 cm, W. 62 cm. Musées royaux d'Art et d'Histoire, Brussels: inv. 319, Evenepöel Collection.

This plaque, quite as celebrated as the dish with the Battle of Vught (Pl. 7), represents an advance in the influence of paintings of the northern school on Dutch faience. The lively style of the kermess is evocative of Breugel. Eighty figures can be counted in this composition. An important clue is given on the sign of the left-hand house: a crescent, the date 1640 and the letters I R. On the roof of the right-hand house is also a sign with a fleur-de-lis and an armorial shield, which if deciphered might be very interesting. The crescent with the date may well not be (as is often thought) the signature and date of this piece but, rather, a faithful rendering of what was on the engraving used as a model. Such cases are known, notably on French faiences.

9 Plaque: delftware, blue-and-white, mark F. v. Frytom (Frederik van Frÿtom also known as Frijtom), dated 1659. H. 62 cm, W. 100 cm. Rijksmuseum, Amsterdam: inv. 475.

This faience picture is of capital importance for our knowledge of the great master Frederik van Frÿtom, not only because of its size but especially because of the signature and the date inscribed at the bottom on the right, on a tree trunk. In fact, this piece is the starting-point for the hypothetical attribution of a certain number of plaques, dishes and even vessels. Since this piece appeared, the same signature has been found on a plaque in a private collection: the name of Frÿtom and the date 1692 (cf. C.H. de Jonge, *Delft Ceramics,* Pl. III, page 193). This 'painting' in the Rijksmuseum that we illustrate here must be regarded as an extraordinary tour de force. The execution of a plaque like this is of enormous technical difficulty, the few places where it has cracked in the kiln are easily explained. Due to the large dimensions of the plaque, the artist was able to achieve all the effects of perspective characteristic of his landscapes.

10 Dish: delftware, blue-and-white, dated 1670. D. 37.5 cm. Rijksmuseum, Amsterdam: inv. 12 400-41.

This dish belongs to a very interesting group, some pieces of which are dated between 1650 and 1675. The decoration is nearly always borrowed from Flemish painting, from Berghem to Van Goyen, from Honthorst to the Teniers. It is David Teniers who inspired this harsh picture of a school: its naturalism has almost turned to caricature. In the Italian manner, the dish displays the painting, while the flat rim is decorated with a simple scroll of flowers and leaves.

The care given to the handling and the national character of the subject are both characteristic of what is often called 'first Dutch porcelain'.

11 Rectangular plaque: delftware, blue-and-white, Frederik van Frÿtom, 2nd half of 17th century. H. 32 cm, L. 38 cm. Musées des Beaux-Arts, Rouen, former Pottier Collection.

While the great plaque (Pl. 9) in the Rijksmuseum is a work of unusual size, one often finds pieces of much smaller dimensions, from 55 to 24 centimetres. The artist used typically Dutch engravings; some writers think that Frederik van Frÿtom composed some himself. The subject treated on the plaque of Plate 9 is an imaginary landscape. Here, on the other hand, it has been possible to identify the very spot portrayed. It is a view of Loenen on the River Vecht. This plaque has not been much illustrated, except by A. Vecht in his book on Van Frÿtom. The painter manipulates a perspective in four planes in a quite astonishing manner; especially remarkable is the way he represents a carefully studied composition of plants in the foreground, a device that he often uses. As often happens with faience decoration, traces of pricking can be discerned, particularly in the hastily drawn birds.

12　Plate: delftware, blue-and-white, school of Frederik van Frÿtom, late 17th century. D. 24.5 cm. Musées royaux d'Art et d'Histoire, Brussels: inv. 131b, Evenepoël Collection.

Frederik van Frÿtom is known to have done more than decorate plaques, and dishes and plates have been attributed to him, as well as a few closed forms. The plates are always decorated in the centre, with the rim left white. Several series are known. The plate illustrated here, for instance, belongs to a set of seven pieces preserved at the same museum. A comparison of the known pieces would probably make it possible to arrive at a better understanding of the various types involved: there is no guarantee that all these plates, even within a series, are the work of a single artist, especially since the compositions are taken from engravings. Almost always, a middle ground of the landscape is placed diagonally, usually on the left, while the other side runs back into a remote distance. The foreground is mostly peopled with a few little, rather insignificant, figures. The drawing in general is distinguished by heavy outlines, unlike many of the pieces that can be attributed to Frederik van Frÿtom with certainty.

13　Plate: delftware, blue-and-white, 2nd half of 17th century. D. 25.5 cm. Rijksmuseum, Amsterdam: inv. 163, Loudon Collection.

Among the works often attributed to Frederik van Frÿtom are several sets with a common theme, such as scenes from the life of Christ, a subject that appears continuously throughout the history of delftware. Often these pieces follow the classical period style of production and carry the decoration in a round medallion surrounded by a plain band, with the rim left empty. The shape is traditional and the delicate tone of the blue is comparable to that tone characteristic of Van Frÿtom. It is set off by relatively fine dark outlines (*trek*). The tin glaze and transparent lead glaze (*kwaart*) produce a very 'porcellanous' effect. The design is evidently a reproduction of the engravings that were widespread during the period, patently Dutch in execution. A rather picturesque note is added by the fact that the various figures, apart from Christ, are dressed in contemporary fashion: a custom that originated in the Middle Ages. This may be an evocation of the feast of Palm Sunday, which at the time was celebrated by a procession in every town in Europe. The background, however, depicts architecture that is in no way northern.

14　Octagonal plaque: delftware, blue-and-white, Frederik van Frÿtom, dated 1662. H. 28 cm. Rijksmuseum, Amsterdam: inv. 17, Loudon Collection.

Among the works that can be attributed to Frederik van Frÿtom belong a certain number of octagonal plaques, perhaps intended to be placed in frames of the same shape. The designs are either landscapes or church interiors, as on the piece illustrated here. The role played by this type of theme in contemporary Dutch painting is well known. The artist succeeds in producing light effects solely by the manipulation of the tones of blue. This series of polygonal pieces is notable for the skilful effect of perspective, enhanced by the shape of the plaque. The subject is from St Mark's gospel, 'the widow's mite'. The reference to the verse and the date, 1662, are inscribed at the foot of the plaque. If this piece is really by Frederik van Frÿtom, it comes quite early in the artist's œuvre.

15

15 Spice box: delftware, blue-and-white, mark S.V.E. (Samuel van Eenhoorn), late 17th century. H. 20 cm, W. 28 cm. Musée national de Céramique, Sèvres: inv. CL. 7474.

This strange shape seems to have been an invention of the factory of Samuel van Eenhoorn. There is a very similar piece in the Musées royaux d'Art et d'Histoire, Brussels. Inside the box there are vertical walls separating compartments in which different spices were to be stored. Some connection can be seen between these pieces and apothecaries' drug jars: the handles of the vessel and lid are in the form of a snake, which is a frequent motif on drug jars. The Brussels piece, however, has simple straight handles on the box and three fruit on top of the lid. The decoration in blue enhanced by manganese is the same on both pieces and represents a Chinese subject. It is typical of Samuel van Eenhoorn. The linking motifs between the Chinese scenes have been claimed as reminiscent of Italian themes.

16 Bottle: delftware, blue-and-white and manganese, mark S.V.E. (Samuel van Eenhoorn), c. 1680. H. 20 cm. Rijksmuseum, Amsterdam: inv. 14 344.

This piece is remarkable for its shape and the purity of its decoration. The origin of the shape is not an easy problem to solve; one may wonder how far it should be sought in the Near East. It stands on a high footed rim, the body of the vase assuming the profile of a bell; the neck is tall and flares at the top. Boldly drawn Chinese motifs stand out on a glaze of exceptional purity and astonishingly white. The piece as a whole, as sometimes happened in the factory of Samuel van Eenhoorn, is so close to the Chinese style that it constitutes a peak of accomplishment. Later periods will no longer achieve such fidelity to the Orient.

17 Tea caddy: delftware, blue-and-white, mark S.V.E. (Samuel van Eenhoorn), late 17th century. H. 27 cm, W. 13 cm. Musée national de Céramique, Sèvres: inv. 12 519, J. Duval Donation.

This rectangular flask is a very special shape. The Chinese scenes reflect faithfully the motifs on many Wanli-period pieces from China; note the 'perforated rock' with the attempts at exotic plants and the 'cloud'. The interplay of blue and manganese gives great decorative strength to the ensemble. The star-shaped group of leaves and flowers in the top right-hand corner with its conventional arrangement is rather strange. The scene of a dignitary walking under a parasol held by a servant perhaps indicates that this piece was intended for some princely personage, an indication reinforced by the appearance of an emblem on the two narrow sides. The interlace surmounted by a royal crown frames an almost indecipherable monogram, which might be that of William.

18   Tulip vase: delftware, blue-and-white, mark A.K. (Adriaen Kocks), *c.* 1690. H. 34 cm, W. 30 cm. Musée national de Céramique, Sèvres: inv. 23 090, Viefville Bequest.

Among the very original forms conceived by the Delft potters for holding flowers are these strange vases on rectangular pedestals with 23 mouths arranged in a fan, flanked on each side by chimeras. The main decorative motifs are skilfully placed on the base: lambrequins (*fransche Punt*) and stylized foliage. Other highly simplified motifs appear on the body of the base placed in such a way that they remain visible when the vase is full. Many combinations of the same sort were elaborated in blue or polychrome with varying numbers of mouths. This piece is among those with the largest number.

18

19

19   Ewer tray: delftware, blue-and-white, mark A.K. (Adriaen Kocks), *c.* 1700. D. 41 cm. Gemeente Museum, The Hague: inv. OC (D) 4.1965.

Following a tradition with origins in the Near East, which reached Italy by way of Spain, this form reappeared at Delft. This large circular tray has a central boss. The decorative composition, however, is entirely Far Eastern in inspiration though it is arranged in a strictly symmetrical radiating pattern. The fantasy is given rein in the centre, decorated with flowers and hooks in reserve on a blue ground. Round it is a ring of 14 *ruyi-*sceptre hearts. This sceptre head 'which exorcises desire' is sometimes used in figure scenes as in China as a decorative motif apart from its literal role there of indicating the carrier's dignity. The cavetto is marked by a double band of fleurons while the flat rim has flowering branches and stylized flowers set alternately in panels.

The interest of a piece like this is to show how far the delftware painter of the great period can impose a classical order on Far Eastern motifs.

20 Dish: delftware, blue-and-white, mark A.K. (Adriaen Kocks), late 17th century. D. 26 cm. Musée national de Céramique, Sèvres: inv. CL. 9 818.

This dish seems inspired by a traditional Italian shape, with the accentuated central hollow and the wide rim. The little putti in reserve on the dense wreath of flowers are also quite classical. The dark outlining (*trek*) is exceptionally thick. It is used not only for the outlines, but for internal details of leaves and flowers: roses, tulips, anemones, etc.; the central figure is not lacking in originality, a woman with her hair streaming in the wind, perhaps symbolizing a season. The Victoria and Albert Museum has a smaller dish of the same form with a very similar rim. Its central motif is a flower vase and a brush pot with a mark that according to William Honey is Samuel van Eenhoorn's. Pieces such as these were perhaps begun in the time of Samuel van Eenhoorn and were continued by Adriaen Kocks in the Greek A factory.

20

21

21 Plate: delftware, blue-and-white, mark A.K. (Adriaen Kocks), *c.* 1690. D. 25 cm. Musée national Adrien Dubouché, Limoges: inv. 969, Gasnault Collection.

This plate is quite a typical example of the attempts made by Dutch designers to compete with the potters of the Far East in odd designs. The composition is exceedingly curious: half with a white ground, half with blue. On the latter, a radiating composition like the branches of a fan stands out in reserve, and cartouches in reserve contain birds and flowers in the Japanese style. The white part is occupied by the image of a fan intended to be very Far Eastern; the painter has even placed in a circle imitation Chinese characters that clearly are meaningless. The blue of this piece is unusually pale compared with the majority of pieces by Adriaen Kocks.

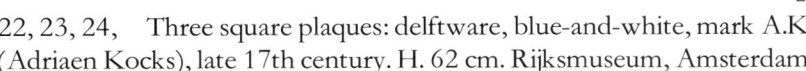

22, 23, 24, Three square plaques: delftware, blue-and-white, mark A.K. (Adriaen Kocks), late 17th century. H. 62 cm. Rijksmuseum, Amsterdam.

This series of plaques, some preserved in the Rijksmuseum and some in the Victoria and Albert Museum (several signed A.K.), formed, according to Arthur Lane, the decoration of a door or fire-place of the dairy or of a small room in the Water Gallery of Hampton Court. As Ida Peelen has already shown in *Catalogus van de kerzameling Nederlandsch Aardwerk,* their decoration is entirely taken from the engravings of Daniel Marot. These engravings are known, and the various decorative elements used as models can be identified. The plaque of Plate 22 is surmounted by the closed crown resting on a dias, the bust of William III of Orange is flanked by two cupids bearing a laurel wreath; Fame floats above this composition. At her left hand the initials W.R. (William Rex) can be seen under a crown.

The plaque of Plate 23 was certainly placed at the bottom of the whole composition. Two pedestals (in the form of terms) are surmounted by baskets of fruit symbolizing the riches of the earth. Two plumed figures evoking court costume lean on a central plinth that supports a vase with elaborate handles. Daniel Marot is known to have drawn vases of this kind to be executed in stone. The draperies, fringes and tassels round the base are typical of the period.

The plaque of Plate 24 must have been at the upper part of the composition, for everything expresses things aerial: music, symbolized by three cupids; two sylphids emerging from a circular frame playing cymbals; the bird, standing in a cage hanging from a dome.

This is the work of Adriaen Kocks. Several authorities have drawn attention to the fact that nothing in the work of this artist was treated with such care and artistry as these plaques.

25

25 Square plaque: delftware, blue-and-white, late 17th century. H. and W. 60 cm. Victoria and Albert Museum, London: inv. C. 13 – 1956.

This additional plaque from Hampton Court, also decorated after the engravings of Daniel Marot, is related to the preceding ones (*cf.* Pls. 22-4) and was part of the same composition. The initials of William and Mary are on the banner hanging from the trumpet played by one of the musicians. The two medallions contain likenesses of the sovereigns.

26 Tulip vase: delftware, blue-and-white, mark A.K. (Adriaen Kocks), late 17th century. H. 100 cm. Hampton Court Palace. Reproduced by gracious permission of Her Majesty Queen Elizabeth II.

The monumental tulip vases designed for Hampton Court are very unusual in conception. Their shape is a tour de force in delftware production of the late seventeenth century; the abundance of the decoration clearly suggests that this was a royal order. Arthur Lane, in an article in *The Connoisseur* (March 1949), demonstrated how it was entirely the invention of Daniel Marot. A visit to the Queen's Gallery at Hampton Court, where these vases are now preserved, is really needed to become aware of the sumptuous effect of all these pieces together.

The tulip vase illustrated here (one of a pair) is among those naming in their inscriptions both William III and Mary II. The construction of the vase consists of a pedestal foot with very simple decoration: a central part in two sections with emblems and other motifs, among them the cyphers of William and Mary (W M R R WILHELMUS Maria Rex Regina); an upper part with devices in cartouches: harp, fleur-de-lis, rose and thistle. Above this ensemble rests the part that holds the tulips, itself divided into two removable sections, with its mouths and a top in the form of a royal crown.

27, 28 Two tulip vases: delftware, blue-and-white, mark A.K. (Adriaen Kocks), late 17th century. Pl. 27: H. 100 cm, Pl. 28: H. 145 cm. Hampton Court Palace. Reproduced by gracious permission of Her Majesty Queen Elizabeth II.

The pieces illustrated here are of the same series as the tulip vase illustrated in Plate 26; Plate 27 also evokes William and Mary. The composition has evident links with other vases with the royal crown, in the ring foot and squat form, but the body is basically composed of a four-sided obelisk. The mouths are set on the edges and adopt the shape of a gaping monster; the lid has a strange knob in the form of a spiral cone.

Many writers have thought the tulip vase of Plate 28, which only has the emblem and effigy of William III, might be slightly later; here already is a composition that was to become traditional. The large plinth is six-sided; above, resting on animals, rise nine storeys of boxes with mouths, forming a pyramid. The decoration with particularly high-quality blue and dark outlines (*trek*) includes an astonishing variety of motifs taken from engravings.

29 Vase with lobed body: delftware, blue-and-white and manganese. H. 48 cm, W. 39 cm. Musée national de Céramique, Sèvres: inv. 22 442.

This form of vase, usually with a domed lid, is also of Oriental derivation. It is one of the types belonging to garniture sets, as will be seen. The decoration is very close to some from the studio of Samuel van Eenhoorn and may be considered contemporary with it. The friezes round the upper and lower parts are a well-known motif. The scene is evidently taken from engravings illustrating contemporary accounts of travels in China. Here, once more, is the famous 'cloud' and conventional trees; great care is given to the depiction of the mandarin's carriage. The figure on the right of the carriage carries the *ruyi* sceptre, indicating his dignity.

30 Vase (originally with lid): delftware, blue-and-white, late 17th century. H. 25 cm. Victoria and Albert Museum, London: inv. C. 23. 71. 1910.

This vase, which certainly originally belonged to a garniture set, is painted in very strong blue. It shows very clearly the way the Delft painter interpreted certain traditional Chinese themes. Here, the famous dragon is transformed into an extravagant bristly chimera with a huge beak, his tail a bird's feather and his back adorned with a volute. His head is turned back to catch what in Chinese tradition should be the 'pearl', which has here become an eight-petalled flower. The monster is pursued by an equally extravagant chimera, in a network of branches and stylized foliage. A dragon of similar type is found on later pieces in the eighteenth century, but treated in a less vigorous style.

The friezes above and below, especially the lower frieze below, are in the same style as the ornament on pieces of 'mixed technique'.

31

31 Vase: delftware, blue-and-white and manganese, *c.* 1690. H. 28 cm. Gemeente Museum, The Hague: inv. OC(D)-x-1953.

Baluster vases are very characteristic of the late seventeenth century. This one is decorated with original Chinese scenes. The figures are still interpreted very faithfully, and the artist is clearly using contemporary Far Eastern models. The strong quality of the blue is set off by a powerful manganese-purple. On many pieces of this kind, the 'lotus panels', decorating the base of the vase also occupy the shoulder or neck. Here, the rocks and bushes seem exceptional. The quality of the decoration brings this work close to the production of the Young Moor's Head factory or the Greek A factory.

32 Wine cup: delftware, blue-and-white, mark P.A.K. (Pieter Adriaensz Kocks), *c.* 1690. H. 7.3 cm. Musée des Arts décoratifs, Paris.

In the experiments made by the Delft potters to imitate the porcelain of the Far East, it happened now and then that, thanks to the perfecting of their technique and the quality of the transparent lead glaze (*kwaart*), they turned out a piece that was particularly striking in its fidelity. It will be noticed that this occurs more easily when the pieces are small, as in the case of this type of cup, intended for drinking wine or tea. The very high quality blue is set off by a brilliant white. The decoration is extremely simplified, seeming to be no more than a pretext for patches of shaded colour.

34

◀ 33   Rectangular plaque: delftware, blue-and-white, dated 1660. H. 17.5 cm, W. 13.5 cm. Musée national Adrien Dubouché, Limoges: inv. 1 006.

Portraits painted on plaques are rare, comprising only a few monarchs and a curious series of faience pictures, of which this is one, preserved in the Rijksmuseum and in this museum at Limoges. M.A. Heukensfeldt-Jansen in the *Bulletin van het Rijksmuseum* has provided the following information: these plaques are effigies of Delft pastors and are taken from engravings by Crispijn van Queborn, copies of paintings by Palamede. The portrait here is of Jean Georges Goethals, pastor at Delft (1611-73). The date 1660 is legible at the bottom left. The blue pigment looks less homogeneous here than is usual at Delft, which may be explained by the rather early date. The attribution can hardly be questioned since all the plaques portray people who lived at Delft.

34   Rectangular plaque: delftware, blue-and-white, late 17th century. H. 24.4 cm, W. 39.9 cm. British Museum, London: inv. A.F. 3 187.

This scene is a faithful reproduction of an engraving by C. Decker, to illustrate a book entitled *Description of the Town of Delft (Beschrijvinge der Stadt Delft)*. It shows the fish market and the meat hall with the butchers' guildhouse at Delft. The painter's treatment is not without naïvety. While it is possible that this plaque is contemporary with the work of Frederik van Frÿtom, there is no disputing that the style is very different. In our opinion, this curious piece should be attributed to an unknown artist. The buildings portrayed still stand today, virtually unchanged.

35 Oval plaque: delftware, blue-and-white, late 17th century. H. 20 cm, W. 28.5 cm. Musée national de Céramique, Sèvres: inv. 4 925.

This oval plaque is one of a pair that has occasioned much study because of the inscriptions on them. The scene here shows Chinese and European ships before a fortified Chinese city. The mate to this plaque, which is frequently illustrated, shows the Battle of La Hogue in Normandy, which took place on 29 May 1692 and in which the French were defeated by the combined English and Dutch fleets. On the back of the piece illustrated here, one can read, in cursive script: *Rit Reinier*. The *Reinier* is just visible on the other plaque, and also *I. Altubon*. Earlier authors identified it as the signature of the Delft potter called Reinier Hey. This hypothesis is no longer accepted today. Experts are agreed that the style of the painting certainly has connections with that of Frederik van Frÿtom.

36 Lidded vase: delftware, 'mixed technique', monogram I.W. (Hoppesteyn factory), late 17th or early 18th century. H. 75 cm. Musée de la Chartreuse, Douai.

This vase and its pendant, which are little known, are quite exceptional pieces among the products of the Hoppesteyns. Several of the most characteristic features of Delft production are combined here. The baluster form with an octagonal base, the dome-shaped lid with a spherical knob are impeccably treated on vases of a size unusual for the Hoppesteyns. The 'mixed technique' decoration comprises a representation on the body of the vase of the court of the emperor (?), portrayed in a very sumptuous manner; very elaborate combinations of decorative motifs adorn the upper and lower parts of the vase and the lid. The lambrequins of the upper register are in every respect comparable to those on Chinese pieces of the Wanli period.

36

37

◀ 37 Handled bottle: delftware, blue-and-white, mark R.I.H.S. (Rochus Jacobsz Hoppesteyn), late 17th century. H. 35 cm. Rijksmuseum, Amsterdam: inv. 5 830.

Of the same high standard as the pieces in 'mixed technique' signed by the master of the Young Moor's Head factory are those treated in blue-and-white bearing the same monogram. The monochrome is compensated for by the abundance of decoration, here arranged in six superposed friezes to show up the swelling profile of the piece. On the base runs a band of the *ruyi*-sceptre motifs favoured by this artist; above is a broad band with contorted Chinese figures among plants and clouds; then comes a belt of scrolls with cartouches in reserve containing similar figures. On the shoulder other figured landscapes are surmounted by a frieze of scrolls. This is a composition where the painter has tried, perhaps not entirely successfully, to accumulate subjects while avoiding heaviness.

38 Vase: delftware, 'mixed technique', mark I.W. (Hoppesteyn factory), late 17th or early 18th century. H. 31 cm. Musée national de Céramique, Sèvres: inv. 22 413.

In the wares decorated in what we have called 'mixed technique', two types can be distinguished according to the main motifs: European or Far Eastern in inspiration. This example is characteristic of how Italian Renaissance painters were copied. The three subjects in blue-and-white, in fact, can be shown to reproduce engravings made by Rubeis after the tapestry cartoons produced by Giulio Romano for the Vatican, with scenes from the life of Constantine: *The Meeting of Constantine and Helen, Pope Sylvester Vanquishing Heresy, The Destruction of the Idols* (illustrated here). The vase clearly comes from a garniture set. It is comparable to the vases in the Evenepoël Collection in the Musées royaux d'Art et d'Histoire, Brussels, whose subjects also come from engravings by the great Italian masters. These scenes are always treated in blue-and-white, and it is the decorative motifs framing them for which enamels and gilding are used.

38

39

39 Jug: delftware, 'mixed technique', monogram R.I.H.S. (Hoppesteyn factory), with the Moor's Head above, late 17th century. H. 24.5 cm. Musées royaux d'Art et d'Histoire, Brussels: inv. 29, Evenepoël Collection.

On an unusually simple shape the artist has placed a very rich decoration: it includes four figures round a low table. Once again the importance of the mandarin is stressed, for he is seated with a servant behind him who bears a *ruyi* sceptre. This receding motif allows the painter to fill a space that might otherwise have remained empty. Beside the handle is another table with various objects and vases on it, which on more ordinary pieces would form the main part of the decoration. The frieze scroll at the top fills a relatively broad band. The use of green and gold is minor compared with the red and blue. This is one of the pieces, not at all numerous, which has the emblem of the Moor's Head, the factory's sign, as well as the mongram R.I.H.S.

40 Dish: delftware, 'mixed technique', mark I.W. (Hoppesteyn factory), late 17th or early 18th century. D. 40.8 cm. British Museum, London: inv. 90.12.13.5.

The rich effects created by the 'mixed technique' attracted orders from the nobility of foreign countries. At least two dishes are known with the arms of the Von Braunschweig family; Arthur Lane found that two members of that family may be involved, either Calenberg or Lüneburg. The Lüneburg branch is known to have been closely connected with Holland and England. On this dish in the British Museum is depicted a military scene from Roman history. The other dish with the same arms (in the Victoria and Albert Museum) represents 'The Rape of the Sabines'. These subjects are taken from the engravings of Galestruzzi, after Polidoro da Caravaggio, which appeared in 1658. Rather unusually, the polychrome decoration of the flat rim, with its putti playing trumpets and its classical scrolls, is markedly European in inspiration.

41   42

41, 42   Two sweetmeat dishes: delftware, 'mixed technique', monogram R.I.H.S. (Hoppesteyn factory), late 17th or early 18th century. H. 19 cm. Rijksmuseum, Amsterdam.

These two dishes come from the same set as the dish with the hunter shown in Plate 43, which is made for rice and its garnishes, called *rijsttafelstel* or sweetmeat dishes in English. The Oriental decoration is treated in polychrome with great verve and is reminiscent of certain half-Chinese, half-Japanese pictures widespread at the time. Some quite un-Oriental motifs are found in certain details, for instance in the motif with pendants adorning the front parts of the robes. The landscapes are lightly sketched, with one bush or a few leaves. The mountains are suggested by no more than a single line.

43   Sweetmeat dish: delftware, 'mixed technique', mark R.I.H.S. (Hoppesteyn factory), late 17th or early 18th century. H. 19 cm, W. 34 cm. Musée national de Céramique, Sèvres: inv. 22 374. ▶

This element of a rice set comes from the same set of dishes (*risjttafelstel*) as the pieces illustrated in Plates 41 and 42. Its companion is also preserved in the same museum. Here, the composition is large and the subject is treated in a way that fits beautifully with the shape of the dish. The scene, a mounted huntsman, recalls pictures in collections that were widely circulated at the time, such as the *Book of Brigands*. The border is a very simple interlace, punctuated by delicate fleurons and heightened with gold. On this dish, as on one of those in the Rijksmuseum, the ground is depicted by sinuous lines of the type normally used for 'clouds'.

44

44 Cream bowl: delftware, 'mixed technique', mark A.K. (Adriaen Kocks), *c.* 1690. D. 47 cm. Victoria and Albert Museum, London: inv. C. 90.1950.

45 Tea caddy: delftware, 'mixed technique', mark A.K. (Adriaen Kocks), *c.* 1690. H. 14.7 cm. Musée national de Céramique, Sèvres: inv. 4 528.

The two cream bowls, one in blue-and-white, the other, illustrated here, with the addition of overglaze enamel colours, are among the best pieces attributed to Adriaen Kocks. Arthur Lane discovered that the designs on these bowls were borrowed from Daniel Marot. The conical shape flares at the rim. The composition is dominated by a certain radiating style, with four panels with trellis-filling separating pastoral scenes. The use of enamels and gilding shows the precious character of an object that is normally rustic. This is explained by Arthur Lane, who found that these were furnished for the dairy of Queen Mary II in the Old Water Gallery at Hampton Court. It is known from many pieces that Adriaen Kocks was the main supplier of pottery to the palace.

This rectangular shape with a metal stopper is typical. Like the Hoppesteyns, Adriaen Kocks sometimes used 'mixed technique', perhaps with a little more simplicity. Here, the inspiration is Far Eastern, as is to be expected for a tea caddy. It consists of flower vases placed on various kinds of stands, each occupying a side framed by a chequered motif. The flowers and leaves are treated in a rather naïve manner with little dabs of the brush creating a stippled effect. The heart-shaped cartouches in reserve are curious, enclosing enigmatic motifs that vaguely recall Buddhist emblems.

45

46

46 Rectangular plaque: delftware, high-temperature polychrome, Gÿsbrecht Verhaast, late 17th century. H. 22 cm, W. 23 cm. Musée national de Céramique, Sèvres: inv. 9 675.

A comparison with the signed pieces (see Pl. 47) enables us unhesitatingly to attribute to Verhaast a number of other plaques (quite rare) inspired by the 'intimist' painting much in vogue in Holland at the time. This is a satirical scene rather curiously composed, and one may wonder if there is not a symbolic idea behind it. Orange-yellow is again given great importance but an exceptionally large part is dominated by white and the blue sky. These pieces are so rare and precious that it has never been possible to make a technical analysis.

47 Rectangular plaque: delftware, high-temperature polychrome, ▶ signed Gÿsbrecht Verhaast, late 17th century. H. 23.5 cm. Musées royaux d'Art et d'Histoire, Brussels: inv. 294, Evenepoël Collection.

The plaques painted by Gÿsbrecht Claesz Verhaast are among the strangest technical feats achieved at Delft during this period. This artist is mentioned about 1689 as a faience potter (literally, 'dishmaker', *plateelbakker*) in the Young Moor's Head factory with Jacob Wemmersz Hoppesteyn. This is surely the explanation of the technical knowledge that enabled him to make these extraordinary attempts to imitate in faience the effects of oil-painting. There is a striking connection with the way glass painters handled colours. The present piece has the artist's signature on the window frame. The scene is of a somewhat common interior in which, as nearly always on pieces by Verhaast, an orange-yellow is dominant.

48

48 Dish: delftware, high-temperature polychrome, late 17th century. D. 31 cm. Musée national de Céramique, Sèvres: inv. 5 797.

49 Plaque with foliate border: delftware, high-temperature polychrome, *c.* 1700. H. 38 cm, W. 33 cm. Musée national Adrien Dubouché, Limoges: inv. 979, Gasnault Collection.

The form of this deep dish with a lobed rim originated in Italy. It belongs to the type of Italian 'white ware' called *bianchi di Faenza,* which appeared in the late sixteenth century, a style that spread throughout Europe during the seventeenth century. These dishes appear to have been produced in abundance in the Netherlands. The decoration, with a limited palette of blue, yellow and green, leaves much space to the white tin glaze. On many pieces of this ware, the centre is occupied by a portrait of William III of Orange (chief of state [*stathouder*] of the United Provinces, 1672-1702, and king of England, 1689-1702), framed by two tulips, while the rim has a wreath of flowers, leaves and fruit. On other pieces of the same shape, the subjects are either directly inspired from Italy or there are patently Dutch figures.

Most writers consider that this type of plaque with flower pieces (*bloemendekor*) can be classed among the first examples of high-temperature polychrome decoration at Delft. The artist can be seen to have achieved great mastery already, succeeding with a very small number of colours: blue, green, yellow, orange, manganese-purple, in giving a superb effect of richness and luminosity. The floral spray is probably taken from an engraving, from which a pricked drawing was made; this is proved by the extraordinarily close similarity between this plaque and the one preserved in the Rijksmuseum, though a few minor differences can be discerned in the placing of the colours. As on many plaques, the rim is raised and painted in what is often called 'manganese-black'.

50

50 Dish, mug and bowl: delftware, white, late 17th or 18th century. Dish: D. 37 cm. Gemeente Museum, The Hague: inv. OCD. 9-1957; OCD. 162-1904; OCD. 77-x-1915.

51 Openwork basket, with lid: delftware, high-temperature polychrome, *c.* 1710. H. 19.5 cm. Gemeente Museum, The Hague: inv. OCD. 145-1904, Van der Burgh Collection.

Following a tendency prevalent in Europe in the early seventeenth century to reduce or suppress all decoration, Delft, particularly at the end of the seventeenth century, produced a large quantity of 'white ware'. The influence of Italian 'white ware' called *bianchi di Faenza* is particularly apparent on the lobed dishes; jugs take very varied forms; the bowl shown here has sometimes been described as a cake mould. The white tradition continued with changes: *blanc de Chine* was copied first and French porcelain later.

This basket is the result of a close combination of European and Oriental styles. The shape, in which the Delft potter exhibits his virtuosity by contriving openwork, which can only be obtained because of the fine quality of the clay, is entirely European. The little creature on the lid, on the other hand, is an imitation of the very popular Chinese motif, the dog of Fo. The decoration, too, is a typical mixture of the two sources of inspiration: the flowers, foliage and chequer pattern are directly related to Sino-Japanese design, while two medallions in reserve hold European scenes treated in blue-and-white. On one side a man and a woman sit drinking; on the other (the side shown here) is a subject from the Gospels that is found on several pieces of delftware: the episode of the woman taken in adultery, when Christ writes on the sand (John VIII: 3-11).

51

52

52 Teapot: Delft red stoneware, mark Ary de Milde, late 17th century. H. 11.5 cm, W. 15.5 cm. Musée national de Céramique, Sèvres: inv. 2 244.

The Dutch factories began a plentiful production of teapots in fine stoneware in Far Eastern style in the seventeenth century. Though other signatures are known in this ware, two seem to be most frequent: Ary-Jansz de Milde and Jacobus de Caluwe. In 1658, Ary de Milde won his certificate of mastership and worked in the Greek A factory. The registration of his mark in 1680 falls in the period of Samuel van Eenhoorn.

Judging by these dates, Ary de Milde can be considered one of the first, if not the first, European maker of red stoneware teapots in the Chinese manner. He was followed by the Germans (Meissen and Bayreuth), the English (Fulham and Staffordshire) and, later, the Frénch (Lille). Several writers note that Tschirnhausen, the collaborator of Böttger at Meissen, visited Delft in 1701; nevertheless, the body of the teapots varies noticeably from one centre to the other.

53

53 Teapot: Delft red stoneware, mark J. de Caluwe, *c.* 1710. H. 16 cm, W. 22 cm. British Museum, London: inv. 91. 4. 14. 24.

The teapot illustrated here is signed by Jacobus de Caluwe who, according to Jean Helbig, was producing this type of pottery before he entered the Guild of St Luke in 1709. He had been appointed shareholder (*winkelhouder*) in 1708. Caluwe took a great deal of trouble with the decoration of his stonewares, and the design consists of moulded floral motifs with many well-formed adornments added. Helbig says that the body of the stonewares of this potter is less hard than that used by Ary-Jansz de Milde. Might it not be possible to conclude that the production of Caluwe followed that of Ary de Milde, who died in 1708?

54

66

54, 55 Tulip vase: delftware, blue-and-white, c.1720. H. 120 cm, W. 28 cm. Musée national de Céramique, Sèvres: inv. 23 091, Viefville Collection.

These two views of a tulip vase enable us to understand how the superposition of boxes was devised. The large rectangular base resting on four feet supports seven square vases. In arranging the pieces in this way, the painter is led to reproduce the same motifs at an ever-reduced scale up to the top cup. It can be seen how the artist places his main design on the pedestal. The modeller often puts all his imagination into composing the mouths that are set at each corner and are given the form of gaping chimera. Of course, the mouths are attached to the base of the box in such a way that the plant is in direct contact with the bottom of the vase. These shapes have been given a variety of names, such as pyramid obelisk, but as Michael Archer reminds us, in the early seventeenth century English inventories spoke of 'flower pyramids'. Their great period is considered to be between 1688 and 1710.

56

56 Garniture set: delftware, high-temperature polychrome, mark W.K. with a number, early 18th century. Central vase: H. 57.5 cm, D. 28.5 cm; flared vase: H. 51 cm, D. 21 cm; gourd vase: H. 43.5 cm, D. 20 cm. Musée national de Céramique, Sèvres: inv. 23 089, Viefville Collection.

This set of five garniture vases conforms to the system of decorative Chinese vases. The decoration is divided into panels and treated with a delicate palette. There are three typical shapes: the baluster vase, the double gourd vase and the polygonal flared vase. A complete set with all its lids is not often to be found. It is interesting to see how skilfully the painter has interpreted his motifs to fit the various shapes, preserving a unity that does no injury to the general fantasy. This set is one of large scale, intended to be displayed on a high shelf or piece of furniture.

57 *Rijsttafelstel*: delftware, high-temperature polychrome, Star mark ▶ (the White Star factory), early 18th century. Total L. 75 cm. Stedelijk Museum 'Het Prinsenhof', Delft.

This set of dishes, in English conventionally termed 'sweetmeat dishes', is a well-known Chinese form. The same idea is behind the shape of pieces that when put together form an emblem, here the water sign. The palette is limited to two colours but the set is still comparable to the piece in Plate 81. Here each dish is edged with a scroll motif, but similarity to the dish of Plate 81 is most striking: note the perching bird which must come from the same pricked drawing. The single star mark (the White Star) is the same as on the dish.

57

58

◀ 58   Garniture set on a cupboard: delftware, high-temperature polychrome, mark L.V.E. (Lambertus van Eenhoorn), 1st half of 18th century. H. 60 cm. Rijksmuseum, Amsterdam: inv. 12 400 - 201/205.

This display in the Rijksmuseum is an excellent example of the way these fine garniture sets were often arranged, for most of these chests were used to display three, five or seven vases, either of Chinese porcelain or delftware. The idea of using vases as architectural decoration was very widespread at the time, not only in Holland but throughout Europe.

59

59   Openwork basket: delftware, Delft *doré, c.* 1690. D. 32 cm. Musées royaux d'Art et d'Histoire, Brussels: inv. 80, Evenepoël Collection.

60

The openwork form required considerable virtuosity on the part of the potter. The scene is treated very differently from the usual manner in Delft *doré*. The subject, a seated figure playing with an animal (cat?) and shaking little bells (?) is rather unexpected. The palette, too, is unusual: generally it is the blue that is set against the gold, but here we find the classical effect of dark red against gold. On both these counts, the arrangement of the palette and the drawing, we are inclined to see this as a work intermediate between the Hoppesteyns and the specialists in Delft *doré*. Stylistically it could well be contemporary with the former. This is the opinion also of Ferrand Hudig and Beatrice Jansen.

60   Spouted vase: delftware, blue-and-white, dated 1703. H. 14.5 cm. Musée national de Céramique, Sèvres: inv. 19 156.

This vessel form seems to be a peculiarity of the Netherlands, and there have been various suggestions about its use, the most convincing by Jean Helbig on the strength of a print representing 'Autumn', engraved by Cock; the print shows one of these vases being used to collect the blood of a slaughtered pig. The vase illustrated here depicts two peasants taking a herd of oxen and pigs to water, perhaps an allusion to the intended purpose of the pot. The date of 1703 on the underside is extremely valuable for defining the style and type of decoration. The dark outlines (*trek*) of the subject are very strong. The scroll motifs on the upper and lower bands and on the handle and spout are very simplified. Inside the vase is a scene in the style of the painter Teniers, showing a man being sick.

61 Brush: delftware, blue-and-white, c. 1720. L. 30 cm. Gemeente Museum, The Hague: inv. OCD. 76 - 1904.

Brush handles in delftware are more common than might be thought. They were the occasion for fanciful motifs at times verging on the odd. Often they are made to suggest the material they would normally be made of, namely horn or ivory. Here we have a curious object with its handle affecting the form of a female body while the other end depicts an animal's head. In two cartouches, on a ground covered with flowers and leaves, are set the busts of a man and a woman, each one beside an urn. Delft was not the only faience centre to make brush handles, but the one illustrated here may be considered to be among the most original.

V THE RAPID RISE IN PRODUCTION IN THE EARLY EIGHTEENTH CENTURY

In the previous chapter we saw the marvellous spirit of invention that gave birth to the art of faience-making at Delft. All was now in readiness for what is sometimes called the golden age of Delft, stretching from about 1690 to 1725.

Several wares can be distinguished, according to the technique and the nature of the decoration. In single-fired, high-temperature wares, blue or polychrome paints were used to depict both European themes and Oriental motifs. The development of 'mixed technique' that took place in the first years of the eighteenth century led to a well-known and distinctive ware known as Delft *doré* (gilded delftware) from the French term. The great potters of this period tended to make all the different types, but it will be seen that two of them made Delft *doré* especially their own. All the potters seem to have been equally at home with European and Far Eastern styles and motifs.

HIGH-TEMPERATURE DECORATION: EUROPEAN DESIGNS

The tradition of blue-and-white continued in all the various factories. Many writers have observed that during this period Dutch motifs tended to recede into the background, but they were never completely abandoned, and religious scenes, taken mostly from the Old and New Testaments, were always popular. The Rose factory produced a signed series of plates with scenes from the life of Christ; the rims are decorated quite distinctively with a frieze of little angels. Plates with interiors can also be found.

Pieces of this type pose dating problems, and opinions are much divided. The mark they carry is either a small Gothic 'r' or the name Roos written in full. In *Delft Ceramics*, De Jonge holds that the former is the mark of the Rose factory at the end of the seventeenth century and the beginning of the eighteenth, and that the latter mark does not appear until the second quarter of the eighteenth century. This implies that that type of piece was produced by the factory over a long period. There are also pieces of the same kind, very rare, with scenes from the engravings of the Dutch artist Hendrick Goltzius, who died in 1616. We know from a dish signed I.V.H. and dated 1729, preserved in the Rijksmuseum, and from another signed similarly and dated 1728, that motifs from an even earlier period were used on ceramics during the first half of the eighteenth century. Indeed, there is no doubt that the influence of Dutch painting never ceased. Some pieces (unmarked), nearly all of which can be dated to about 1720, display seascapes, genre scenes, interiors, etc.

A rather special type of high-temperature faience, which is not always mentioned, is essentially European and shows the importance of the French market for delftware. A whole series of pieces (most of them marked A.R.) was clearly made for France; many pieces have inscriptions in French. One style of dishes and plates is decorated with picturesque figures from everyday life: pedlars, tradesmen, acrobats, riders, each with a caption, such as *Le vendeur de melon* (the melon vendor). Another style, called *assiettes parlantes* ('talking' plates), displays an inscription framed by a frieze—usually a few verses of a somewhat ribald song. These are found in blue-and-white, but most often there is restrained use of other colours as well.

Many of these pieces, then, are marked A.R. We have already mentioned this enigmatic monogram more than once in connection with both high-temperature wares and Delft *doré*. This mark continued in use for a long time. A plate decorated in four colours, preserved in the Musées royaux d'Art et d'Histoire, Brussels (Helbig,

Fig. 144), has A.R. on the back and below that the date, 1719. It is in Oriental style. Other pieces can be dated to around 1730 by the coats of arms they bear. This has led J. Helbig to declare that this potter's 'work dates between 1690 and 1739'. He observes that the attribution to one Augustyn van Reijgersbergen, or Reygens, who owned the Two Wild Men factory in 1661 and then the Golden Boat factory in 1663, cannot be sustained, because Van Reijgersbergen fled from Delft in 1666 with his wife, probably because of embezzlement. It seems wisest to leave the mark unattributed. Earlier it was hoped to link it with a Frenchman, A. Révérend, but since Henry Havard's work that hypothesis has been abandoned.

Among the pieces decorated in the European style, a special place should be kept for those with coats of arms or emblems. They may be in blue-and-white or polychrome; some of them have a remarkable range of colours. While the decoration framing the coat of arms sometimes follows the classical tradition (with scrolls and cherubs), there are many pieces on which some Chinese influence can be felt. The taste for Oriental art was as strong as ever.

Pl. 69
Pl. 67

Pl. 70

HIGH-TEMPERATURE DECORATION: FAR EASTERN STYLE

The factories most inclined to use Oriental themes included the Metal Pot factory with Lambertus van Eenhoorn, the Double Tankard factory with Louwÿs Victorsz (or Fictorsz) and the Rose factory, already cited, whose origins go back to 1660.

Pl. 71

Lambertus van Eenhoorn, of the great faience family, took over the Metal Pot factory from Lambertus Cleffius in 1691. He kept it until his death in 1721. The confusion in distinguishing the mark of Lambertus von Eenhoorn from that of Louwÿs Victorsz is unimportant once we realize that the work of these two potters is similar in every way. It may be impossible to decide who was the inventor of the 'cashmere' motif, but certainly many pieces with this decoration bear the signature L.V.E. The term 'cashmere' was evidently adopted to describe the motif with its iridescent effect, because it calls to mind Indian fabrics with very dense and vigorous motifs. The composition of these designs seems to follow the same principles as were followed in China: a vase has its sides decorated with variegated birds perched on flowering sprays, while the base and shoulder are ringed by friezes of lacey lambrequins. On plates the composition is arranged in a radiating pattern similar to Rouen designs. This 'cashmere' decoration is found on pieces marked P.A.K., but the range of colours is not quite the same.

Pl. 72

Pls. 73-6
Pls. 56, 58, 78
Pls. 77, 80

Pl. 79

Far Eastern types of decoration continued to be popular. At this period the style changed, moving on from imitations of Chinese Wanli-period to Kangxi-period wares. The new freedom released by this change of fashion combined a sometimes dizzy abundance of vegetation with extraordinary flights of fancy. There are many pieces on which the white ground is almost completely submerged by the decoration. This taste for luxuriant decoration no doubt encouraged the painters to use a bright, if limited, palette. It began with two-colour ware, in blue and red; then five-colour painting emerged, with golden yellow, green and black added to the blue and red.

Pl. 80

Pls. 71-3, 75-6, 79

Pl. 81

Several authorities give the Rose factory priority in the use of polychrome decoration. A famous piece is the bottle in the Rijksmuseum, which takes its motifs from Asia Minor. It seems to be unique. The motifs used in polychrome painting in the Rose factory are usually a faithful reflection of Chinese *famille verte* ware of the Kangxi period (1662-1722) that are decorated with a varied palette: different greens, a very intense black and sometimes gold are used with an enamel blue that replaced the traditional underglaze cobalt blue. The centre of these remarkable dishes is filled with dragons (*xilin*) and phoenixes (*fenghuang*). The cavetto has a frieze of chimeras sporting in fantastic landscapes; the rim has cartouches in reserve and green trellises. Many pieces from the same factory are decorated in rich polychrome, usually with Far Eastern scenes.

Pl. 83

Pl. 91

Pl. 86

Other factories deserve some mention: those of Willem Cleffius, of Pieter Adriaensz Kocks and of the enigmatic signatory of the mark A.R. A few important dates concerning Pieter Adriaensz Kocks are known, and here the famous Greek A factory plays a part. This faience potter was the son of Adriaen Kocks, whom he succeeded as owner and shareholder (*winkelhouder*) in 1701. Pieter died in 1703. If we now are to attribute the many pieces with the mark P.A.K. to him, and not (as previously) to Adriaen Pijnacker, we must suppose that the mark was carried on by his widow, who continued at the factory with the assistance of master potters until 1722.

Certain pieces on which there is a strange mingling of Far Eastern with European styles are not too easy to date. A very curious example is the tray in the Musée national de Céramique, Sèvres, with a picture of a black servant handing a cup of chocolate to a lady wearing a fontange head-dress.

It is possible to see a gradual development of style in the depiction of figures, from the early eighteenth century onward, as the Chinese style slowly undergoes transition to the Japanese. We have to go back beyond the turn of the eighteenth century to find the first appearance of those graceful figures (generally female) with their elongated proportions that allowed the painter such elegant curves. The Dutch called them *lange lijsen*, and they have sometimes been called 'long Elizas' in English, though latterly 'slender ladies', or 'beauties', a translation of *meiren*, the Chinese name for them, is more usual. This type of figure remained in vogue during most of the eighteenth century; gradually, however, Japanese influence introduced a rather different type, and created a taste for portraying children and other figures. Certain themes from Japanese Imari ware (porcelain made at Arita for export and shipped from the port of Imari) became popular throughout Europe, for instance sprays of flowers, hedges and a rock pierced with holes, known as a 'perforated rock'.

COLOURED GROUNDS

In following the history of coloured wares in the early eighteenth century, we must set aside a special place for the famous black and brown grounds. They were normally achieved with a coloured glaze. Once again the incentive was the desire to imitate popular imported wares, in this case the Kangxi-period biscuit wares, decorated in imitation of lacquer.

Painting on black glaze was a very delicate operation and must have required special manipulation of the colours. The richest polychrome decoration consists of yellow, red, manganese-purple, sky blue and emerald green. This rich palette occurs complete only on exceptional pieces. It should be noted that it comes very close to the colour range of glass painting. Often fewer colours were used, perhaps two colours on a black ground.

As well as the black ground there are two other grounds, often called 'chocolate' and 'olive'. They generally are only decorated in yellow, though a few rare pieces are cited with more than one colour on an 'olive'

ground. Lieven van Dalen was the great practitioner in this ware; he was the owner of the Young Moor's Head factory, which he bought from Rochus Jacobsz Hoppesteyn in 1692. Van Dalen's monogram is L.V.D. The designs on this ware are always very slight and in yellow; the body is brownish, rather similar to red stoneware. These wares with coloured grounds are not to be confused with a ware on which the ordinary white surface is painted black. The back (of a bowl for instance) then has the ordinary white ground. Many pieces of the latter ware have the mark P.A.K., while some black-glazed pieces, such as a tea caddy in the Victoria and Albert Museum, have the mark attributed to Lambertus van Eenhoorn.

DELFT *DORÉ*

It is customary to classify under the term Delft *doré* a category of wares that are related in their technique to some products by the Hoppesteyns. A piece of blue-and-white is taken by a painter and a certain number of low-temperature colours added, particularly pink and also some gold. It is agreed that the style of the majority of these pieces shows the influence—amounting sometimes to slavish imitation—of the motifs employed by the Japanese Kakiemon family at Imari. The most frequent are a flowering branch and bird, a vase on a table, a flowering hedge or a cock. There are also a leopard and, most often, the 'slender ladies', generally in the company of children at play.

Japanese influence is particularly striking on pieces with 'brocaded' decoration. These are generally polygonal dishes, with a vase of chrysanthemums in the centre, and the overall design is a faithful rendering of what is known as 'old Japan': asymmetrical, rather sparse flower and figure motifs enhancing a prominent white ground; the elements are painted in overglaze enamel colours, particularly red and gold. This is a very common Japanese decoration in the ware attributed to the Kakiemon family, which must have had considerable success in Europe, since it was copied in so many factories in both faience and porcelain. Whether the model was purely Japanese is a moot point. Daisy Lion-Goldschmidt has pointed out in *Poteries et porcelaines chinoises* that China, in order to compete with Japanese exports 'also combined underglaze blue with iron red and gold....' She shows, for example, that the 'flower basket' motif is 'the characteristic Chinese motif....' Also (but more rarely), the zigzag bridge called the 'lightning' motif (*bliksem dekor*) occurs, though it is better known in high-temperature decoration. Some strange bowls preserved in the Musée des Beaux-Arts, Lille, have a head surrounded by rays symbolizing the sun. They have the A.R. mark.

Once again the so-called armorial services, sets of dishes decorated with a coat of arms, have to be put in a special class. Some of the most illustrious coats of arms of the period are found on this ware, among them those of King Frederick I of Prussia; of Louis Alexandre of Bourbon, Count of Toulouse, Admiral of France (1683-1737); of Nicolas Auguste de la Baume, Marshal of France in 1703, Knight of the Holy Spirit in 1705, who died in 1716. His arms on the service allow it to be dated between 1705 and 1716. Another obviously very important service, in which the centre of each piece is painted with the royal arms of England, celebrated the accession of King George I in 1714. There are also some rare examples in this technique of European subjects, even of mythological ones, such as the famous dish with the 'Rape of Europa', in the Rijksmuseum.

Many pieces of this type are marked P.A.K., some others A.R. It can be proved that other factories also made such items. The mark L.V.E. is sometimes found, but rarely.

ENAMELLING: LOW-TEMPERATURE DECORATION APPLIED OVER THE GLAZE

Decorations entirely in overglaze (*petit feu*) enamels are of several kinds. It can easily be established that as far as those in Japanese style are concerned, the artists used the same stencils as for Delft *doré*. It becomes clear that no real chronological distinction can be made between Delft *doré* in the Oriental style and enamelled ware. Indeed, enamelled pieces sometimes occur with the marks P.A.K. or A.R.

All authorities agree in dating to about 1725 the appearance of decoration executed entirely in overglaze technique. As we saw on page 18, the earliest faiences decorated in this way are similar in every way to Delft *doré*, except that high-temperature blue is no longer used. A large number of examples exists with simple designs of flowers and birds, as well as armorial pieces, evidently inspired by East India Company wares. The painters sometimes ventured to create more unusual subjects, for instance the large dishes and plates adorned with a princess on horseback with her retinue, marked A.R. Drug jars were also produced.

Early in the second half of the eighteenth century, we shall see how the muffle-firing (*petit feu*) technique still continued but was generally applied to work of quite a different style.

SHAPES

In the first quarter of the eighteenth century, almost all the shapes of the preceding period continued to be made, and there were few changes. At the most, the appearance of certain motifs in relief are worthy of note, such as a shell at the base of an obelisk or other features, which tended to herald some progress in work with moulds.

The shapes of service pieces were on the increase. At this time, the curious coffee-pot appeared with its conical body and sharply angled spout. Also introduced were the double cruet for oil and vinegar; the cooler, sometimes containing bottles; the fruit dish on a footed stand; the cream pan; the salt cellar; the warmer; the sauce boat; as well as knife and fork handles. There are also fountains, lidded basins, inkstands and money-boxes. It is worth observing that many pieces decorated in Delft *doré*, with their rather characteristic Oriental style, are, nonetheless, entirely European in shape.

62

62   Plate: delftware, blue-and-white, mark Roos (Rose factory), 1st quarter of 18th century. D. 22.4 cm. Gemeente Museum, The Hague: inv. OCD. 57 - 1904, Van der Burgh Collection.

The Rose factory seems to have specialized in a certain type of dish of classic form, treated in a very special manner. The rim is always the same: a frieze of clouds and cupids, two of which hold a wreath above a third at the top, and two others hold crossed palm fronds at the bottom. The cupid frieze is painted in a rather unusual way for Delft. The subjects in the centre of the plate are taken from engravings and painted with exceptional care. It is likely that these pieces were very popular, and production continued for a long period, as shown by changes in the style of the mark from a Gothic r, to Roos written out in full. The marks always signify the Rose factory.

63   Jug: delftware, blue-and-white, mark small Gothic 'r' (Rose factory), *c.* 1720. H. 22.9 cm. Victoria and Albert Museum, London: inv. 1004-1853.

This very famous jug has several different types of decoration and belongs to the series showing pictures that include drapery, tassels and ladies with fontange head-dresses (tall head-dresses of metal, cloth and false curls, as worn by the mistress of Louis XIV, Mlle de Fontanges). Here, a musical scene is depicted, with a strange figure in Oriental costume; two Chinese vases and a tripod create perspective. Friezes occupy the base and shoulder; the band on the latter, with its curled leaves, and the motif on the neck, with a rural scene, are treated in classical style. An elegant volute twines over the handle.

63

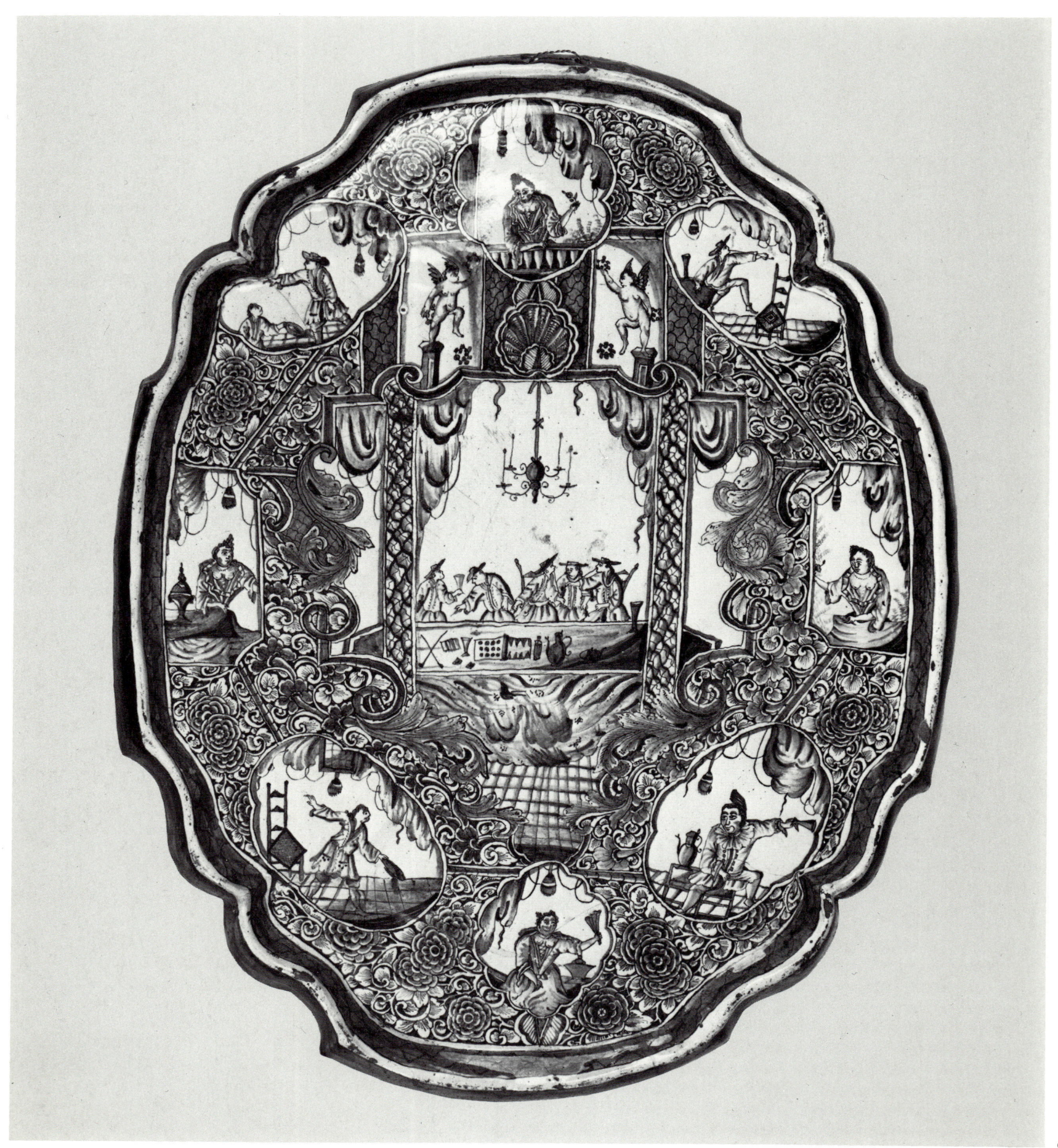

◀ 64   Plaque with indented outline: delftware, blue-and-white, c. 1730. H. 58 cm. Musée des Arts décoratifs, Paris: inv. D. 23 341.

This curious decorative plaque with indented outline has various known motifs of different types. The ground is covered with scrolls and flowers. (This type of ground also occurs on polychrome pieces.) The genre scenes are picked out against cartouches reserved in white and are to be compared with the polychrome dish of Plate 82. In each piece, we find the effects of drapery, paving in perspective and tassels. There is much reference to the smoking den, with marked humour. It is easy to imagine such a piece on the walls of a tavern. There is also a suggestion of influence from contemporary theatre.

65

65   Dish: delftware, high-temperature polychrome, mark A.R., 2nd quarter of 18th century. D. 35 cm. Musée national de Céramique, Sèvres: inv. 19 132.

So far no one has been able to discover the name of the man with the monogram A.R. The mark appears on a quite large group of pieces made especially for France, decorated either with representations of the various handicrafts with an inscription in French or else with more or less scurrilous couplets in French. There are many figures of actors, of mountebanks or, as here, of the 'Cries of Paris'. Some are in blue-and-white, but most are in a quite discreet polychrome. Most of these pieces are preserved in French museums; we have named them 'French delftware'.

66   Dish: delftware, blue-and-white, mark r (Rose factory), c. 1720. D. 29 cm. Musée national Adrien Dubouché, Limoges: inv. 974.

This form of dish with a slightly lobed edge is relatively rare for delftware. The scene with figures is treated overall according to a method not unusual at Delft. Two types of painting are combined: the two groups of figures in the centre, doubtless taken from engravings, are drawn in dark outlines (trek) with precision, whereas the rocky landscape is very freely painted; on pieces of this kind it even happens that the design is applied without drawing, sometimes referred to as sponged technique. This same ware can occur with slight additions of colour.

66

67 Plate: delftware, blue-and-white, mark C.W., 1st half of 18th century. D. 22.5 cm. Musée national Adrien Dubouché, Limoges: inv. 961, Gasnault Collection.

This armorial plate has a border of fleur-de-lis, which links it with certain Delft *doré* pieces, but the treatment, here in blue-and-white, is much simpler. The oval shield surmounted by a comital crown and flanked by two palmettes is filled with a device that should be decipherable: a dove with an olive branch perched on Noah's ark.

On the back are three concentric blue lines and the mark C.W., as yet unexplained.

68 Plate: delftware, blue-and-white, early 18th century. D. 21.5 cm. Musée national Adrien Dubouché, Limoges: inv. 1 009, Gasnault Collection.

This plate with the portrait of Louis XV as a child is not widely known but is certainly very interesting. The inscription *Lodtroyk dù rooy de Franst 1715* (King Louis of France, 1715) marks a period of peace between Holland and France and the accession of the new king. The circular medallion has the frequently seen motif of tasselled curtains and a house with a curved gable in the northern manner. The design on the rim, with its birds in scrolls in reserve on a blue ground and flowers in cartouches, is extremely simple.

69 Plate: delftware, high-temperature polychrome, dated 1704. D. 25.5 cm. Musées royaux d'Art et d'Histoire, Brussels: inv. 463, Evenepoël Collection.

This plate (one of a pair) is typical of a rather special series which can be placed easily in the history of armorial delftware, because it is dated 1704. The polychrome painting is of unusual quality, the colours on the bottom of the dish standing out against a black ground. A certain translucence in the glazes creates an effect not unlike painting on glass. The shield surmounted by a helmet is crowned in a strange manner by a human bust. The lambrequins of the crest resemble leaves. The alternating full and reserve lacy scroll motifs on the flat rim are separated from the central motif by a very simple line of hatching on the cavetto, broken by the inscription of the name of the man for whom the plate was made, Jan Kownsown (?), and the date 1704.

70 Dish: delftware, blue-and-white, mark J.B. and a star (Johannes de Bergh ?), late 18th century. D. 26 cm. Musée national de Céramique, Sèvres: inv. 3 855.

Blue-and-white armorial pieces are found throughout the eighteenth century. The absence of other colours is sometimes, as here, compensated for by the richness of the decorative motifs. The two shields of the betrothal are set against what was normally a *plume* or mantling, which is here so profuse that it has become purely decorative. The rim is still classical in inspiration, with foliage and festoons, medallions and cherub heads in the manner of Daniel Marot. There has been some disagreement about this dish: A. Demmin, in *Histoire de la céramique* (1868-75), on the basis of the arms, wanted to date this piece to the sixteenth century, but Henry Havard convincingly demonstrated the improbability of such a hypothesis. The initials J.B. accompanying the star, which appears to indicate the White Star factory, give rise to some doubt in attribution. It is generally assumed that they are of Johannes de Bergh, who was master in the factory from 1772 to 1776, which gives a strangely late date to these pieces, considering their style.

71 Dish: delftware, blue-and-white, mark L.V.E. (Lambertus van Eenhoorn or Louwÿs Victorsz). D. 44 cm. Gemeente Museum, The Hague; inv. OCD. 37 1904, Van der Burgh Collection.

There are many dishes imitating very faithfully a classic type of Chinese ware of the Wanli period, which was widespread in Europe. It is possible that this production began in the Netherlands before it did at Delft. It is generally dated to a period between 1650 and 1700.

The composition varies in detail, but the principal lines are unchanging: a main subject occupies the centre; it is framed by an irregularly shaped eight-sided band; the rim and cavetto have alternating panels enclosing highly stylized 'precious objects'. The blue of these pieces is nearly always very strong. It should be borne in mind that the Dutch factories were not alone in producing this type of dish. They are also found at Hanau and Frankfurt in Germany.

72 Dish: delftware, blue-and-white, mark L.V.E.–K.G. (Lambertus van Eenhoorn), *c.* 1700. D. 26 cm. Musée des Arts décoratifs, Paris: inv. D. 23 320.

This dish is a very striking example of the full decoration quite often found on the wares with the mark L.V.E. In the centre is one of those traditional scenes of birds perching on marsh plants. What is important is the luxuriance of the frame of this motif, very skilfully executed and still quite close to the ideas of primitive delftware. Starting from the dish and stretching right out to the edge of the rim, a rather complex structure is developed. It consists basically of four 'hooks' from which grow what we might call heather leaves; two leaves form brackets to frame the central motif; two leaves curve on to the rim. A close scatter of flowers and foliage, tulip-shaped fleurons, occupies every available space. Round the edge we find brocade motifs in heart shapes, palmettes and scrolls. Often in this factory the blue-and-white decoration is compensated for in lack of other colours by the great richness of the design. On the back of the plate, besides the mark, are four blue dots repeated five times.

72

73 Lidded vase: delftware, blue-and-white, mark G.K. (Gerrit Pietersz Kam), early 18th century. H. 22 cm. Victoria and Albert Museum, London: inv. 44 1887.

This vase was certainly part of a garniture set. It is unusual in having kept its tapered lid. The shape retains all the purity of its Far Eastern origin. Its style fits well in the period 1679 to 1705, when Gerrit Pietersz Kam was working at the Three Ash Barrels factory. The scatter of branches and flowers enlivened with birds, which aimed to leave no empty space on the surface of the piece, confirms the old principle that prolific decoration is a characteristic of primitive pieces. The frieze on the shoulder is also very large. Only round the base do the simple fleurons allow more of the glaze to show. A certain number of pieces are known with similar decoration: almost all are signed G.K.

73

74 Cooler with two bottles: delftware, high-temperature polychrome, mark L.V.E. (Lambertus van Eenhoorn or Louwÿs Victorsz), c. 1700. H. 31 cm., W. 24 cm. Rijksmuseum, Amsterdam.

A few pieces of this type are known. The pair of footed bottles are flat on one side so as to fit together in the basket-shaped basin. This has two mascarons of bearded heads crowned with a plaited handle and a partition separating the two bottles. Other examples are known, mostly in blue-and-white and with other marks, proving that this form was not the speciality of one factory. It is clearly a reproduction of a metal form of the time. Here, the palette consists of blue, red, orange, yellow and green. The basin and one face of the bottles are in a style that can be called classical, very much influenced by the ideas of Daniel Marot. There are alternating motifs, in colour on a white ground and in reserve on a blue ground, similar to the lambrequins at Rouen. The flat part of the bottles shows the other decorative source beloved of delftware, the Far Eastern, with the motif of a panther at the foot of a flowering bush. The piece is marked L.V.E.

74

85

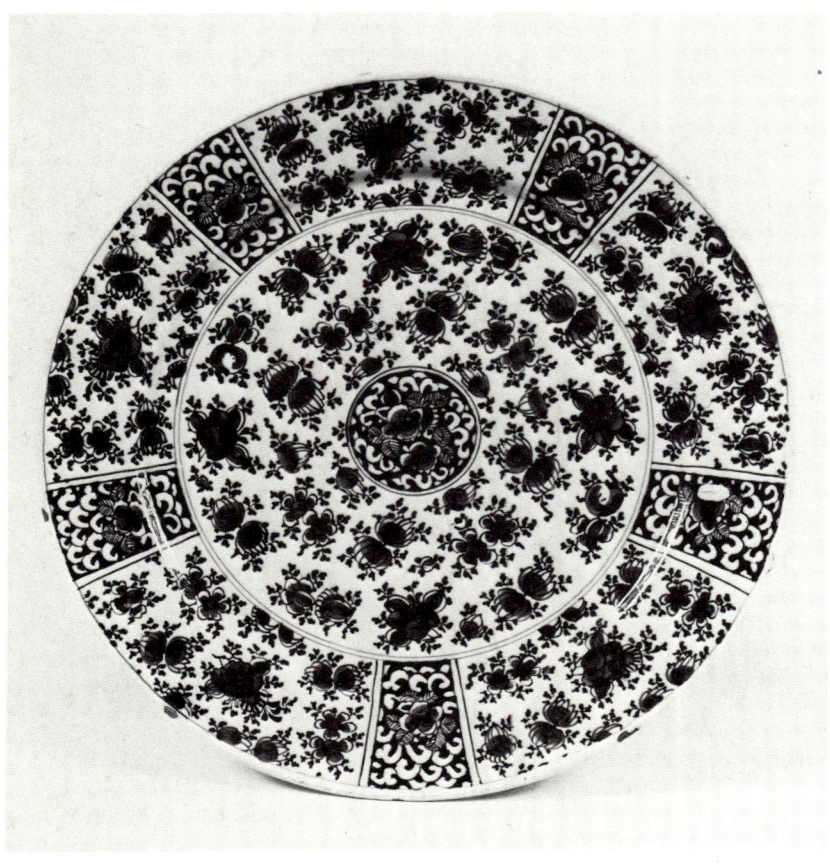

75 Plate: delftware, blue-and-white, mark Roos (Rose factory), *c*. 1730. D. 26 cm. Musée national de Céramique, Sèvres: inv. 5 745.

This broad-rimmed plate is a good illustration of the persistence of certain decorative systems, such as the flower scatter. Here the composition follows the radiating principle— in the centre, a circular medallion; on the cavetto and rim, five identical vertical bands interrupt the scatter. According to De Jonge, the mark Roos, written in full, does not occur earlier than 1727. Several factories seem to have practised the same style during virtually the whole first half of the eighteenth century.

76 Dish: delftware, blue-and-white, mark G.K. (Gerrit Pietersz Kam ?), early 18th century. D. 30 cm. Victoria and Albert Museum, London: inv. 23. 76. 1910.

This type of dish can be linked with the seventeenth-century tradition in its choice of a compartmented design for the cavetto and rim. This forms a frame for a waterscape with ducks painted almost realistically, swooping over a rock overgrown with flowers: the usual 'perforated rock' has in fact been transformed into a flowery rock, with a scatter of little flowers left in reserve. The generously applied dark outlines *(trek)* make the design even more forceful. This type of waterscape certainly influenced the makers of faience at the French factory of Sinceny.

75

76

77 Lidded jar: delftware, high-temperature polychrome, mark WK monogram, early 18th century. H. 57.5 cm. Musée national de Céramique, Sèvres: inv. 23 089.

This vase belongs to the garniture shown in Plate 56. It is a perfect example of one style of the Delft potter during the period when he wished to copy Chinese pieces and his own style was intruding. The very slender form consists of a fluted body with eight panels separated by ribs. The decoration follows the rules for five-colour ware with blue, green, golden yellow and orange-yellow enhanced by the white of the ground. Following the division into panels, the decoration consists of a flowering branch rising from a rock with birds perched on it, alternating with a curiously complex composition: a fantasy landscape with rocks and a stylized willow is bounded above and below by an orange chequered pattern. On the chequer motif are emblems reminiscent of the 'precious objects' painted in blue, stressing the Chinese character of the design. On shoulder and base are lambrequin motifs with flowers and leaves, and the lid has similar decoration. The painting is all broadly executed, and it is understandable that a miniature style was to be avoided for all these motifs distributed on an uneven surface. The monogram WK signed in blue above the figure 8 indicates, as on other pieces, that the attribution of this mark to Willem Cleffius cannot be upheld. His dates of production, between 1662 and 1668, are too early for this type of decoration.

78 79

78 Teapot on stand: delftware, blue-and-white, early 18th century. H. 30 cm. Gemeente Museum, The Hague: inv. OCD. 4 – 1971.

This form of teapot with flattened profile and stiff upright handle, standing on a tripod warmer, is typically European. The origin is almost certainly to be found in contemporary metalwork, and it is interesting that this production is almost contemporary with the red stoneware teapots that are considered the best vessels for making tea. This leads one to suppose that this kind of object, with its decoration, was ornamental rather than utilitarian. Once more we find a Sino-Japanese design (children playing) applied to a European shape.

79 Bottle: delftware, high-temperature polychrome, mark L.V.E. (Lambertus van Eenhoorn), c.1720. H. 20.5 cm. Musée des Arts décoratifs, Paris: inv. D. 23 357.

This type of small bottle with facets turned in towards the base and a knob on the neck is surely taken from metalwork. The intensity of the colours: blue, red, yellow and green gives the piece great richness. The motifs follow the shape quite closely. On this face: a pagoda and perching bird above fantastic flowers. On the other side: a kind of 'perforated rock' with spiral motifs suggesting the water sign. The lambrequins on the neck are very like those on contemporary Chinese pieces.

80 Oval basin: delftware, high-temperature polychrome, mark L.V.E. (Lambertus van Eenhoorn), c.1720. L. 30 cm, W. 24.5 cm. Musée national de Céramique, Sèvres: inv. CL 7 478.

This type of basin is generally accompanied by a ewer. The gadrooned flat rim was often produced by this factory. The palette includes blue, red and few touches of green, but the general impression is of 'red and blue', the two-colour effect that was so much used at Rouen. The Far Eastern influence is very strong. The bottom has a composition of a number of objects in the Chinese manner: vases of flowers, a lidded vase and a picture, all framed in an oval wreath of leaves and flowers. On the rim appears the *système rayonnant* [the 'radiating style', typical of Louis XIV design, was developed at Rouen], with garlands hanging towards the centre to stress the 'system'. The outer border has a motif that does not seem Far Eastern. It is quite frequent on Delft pieces. A blue spiral winds round a ground of red scales. The light touches of green are restricted to stressing a few leaves. The mark L.V.E. superimposing the numbers 3 and 0 is often found in blue or in red.

88

80

81

82

81 Dish: delftware, high-temperature polychrome, early 18th century. D. 24 cm. Victoria and Albert Museum, London: inv. 141. 1887.

Though the shape of this little dish is classically European, with its flat rim and low cavetto, writers are agreed in dating this type of piece to the very early eighteenth century. The all-over decoration is very rich, both in motifs and in palette. Plants and parrots are distributed round a rock. The blue, manganese, orange-red, yellow and olive-green are enhanced by touches of black on the birds' beaks, on some branches and in the hearts of the flowers.

W. B. Honey, in his famous dictionary *European Ceramic Art,* illustrates this piece and compares it with some Rouen wares. This is valid for the parrots, but not for the strange tulip-like flowers; the two wares must be seen as contemporary.

82 Dish: delftware, high-temperature polychrome, *c.*1720. D. 48 cm. Musée national de Céramique, Sèvres: inv. 21 926.

Some European subjects are strangely impregnated with Far Eastern influence. This is particularly noticeable on those rather rare polychrome pieces, featuring blue, red, yellow and green. An engraving clearly was used here by the painter, but his interpretation has a special character. The scene of the little black page serving light refreshment to a fine lady, who wears a fontange head-dress, is a theme often used not only in painting but for figurines (especially Meissen). The composition has the typical paving in perspective and curtains. All this recurs on Rouen pieces and especially with the great faience painter Chapelle. It is amusing to see the strange mixture of sources in the furniture, which is supposed to be European but contains two little tables, one with flowers, that are patently Chinese. The figure of the lady is simply drawn in red. The fontange headdress went out of fashion at the French court in 1713 but was certainly continued longer in Holland; it gives the figure a look similar to the Chinese 'beauties' or 'slender ladies' (*meiren*).

83 Vase: delftware, high-temperature polychrome, mark Roos (Rose factory), *c.* 1700. H. 22.5 cm. Rijksmuseum, Amsterdam: inv. 11 628.

This is a famous piece, distinguished not only by its profile but by its type of decoration. It is not without similarities to the bottle of Plate 15, but it differs by having a low foot and fluted body. As often in the great period of polychrome decoration from the Rose factory, the palette is very rich: blue, red, green, yellow, manganese-purple. Exceptionally, the motifs are curiously reminiscent of Turkish themes. This impression is probably derived from certain rather unusual features: the value of the red similar to the 'tomato red' of Iznik, the presence of motifs like the 'burst pomegranate', the fleurons, the very symmetrical composition to which the painter subjects his plants and flowers with great rigour.

84 Dish: delftware, high-temperature polychrome, 2nd quarter of 18th century. D. 25 cm. Rijksmuseum, Amsterdam: inv. 350.

There is a tendency to date to the second quarter of the eighteenth century the appearance of a new type of motif characterized by the presence of figures of very tall 'slender ladies'. Their height is further stressed by their high hair arrangement, similar to that on the Chinese 'beauties' (*meiren*) so frequently depicted on Kangxi-period *famille verte* vases in porcelain. The division of the composition by the screen and bands is like that found on some faience dishes from Rouen. The same can be said of the rim decoration, with flowers and shells alternating on a scale ground. The palette includes a manganese-purple of great brilliance. A few touches of black, especially on the hair, set off the colours.

85 Plate: delftware, high-temperature polychrome, 2nd quarter of 18th century. D. 13 cm. Private collection.

On very small pieces, the Delft painter may take the opportunity to work as a miniaturist. The little Japanese scene in the centre shows a figure seated on a curved tree trunk of the type found on Imari ware and threatening an emerald green leopard with a whip. The rim is done with little flowers on a white ground, alternating with volutes containing a field of yellow dotted with red. The palette is exquisite, with blue, red, yellow, green and pale manganese-purple.

86 Dish: delftware, high-temperature polychrome, mark Roos (Rose factory), *c.* 1710. D. 40 cm. Rijksmuseum, Amsterdam: inv. 12 400-161.

Several dishes of this type are known in various sizes, with very rich decoration directly inspired by Chinese *famille verte* ware. On each of the known pieces, the central motif and the rim decoration are always the same: on the bottom, in a conventional landscape, a kind of chimera (*qilin*, the Chinese unicorn) confronts the 'phoenix' (*fenghuang*) which is flying in the clouds. Here the scene is framed in a circular medallion decorated with flowers in reserve; on some other pieces there is only a fillet. The flat rim and the cavetto are occupied by an extraordinary frieze composed of four cartouches divided irregularly; in each of these are opposed a monster and a bird, all different. These chimerical beasts are in many cases close to those often represented by Adam Friedrich von Löwenfinck, at Meissen and the other centres where he worked. The edge of the rim, decorated with flowers in reserve similar to those of the circular medallion, is lobed. On other pieces of the same type (for example, in the Boymans van Beuningen Museum, Rotterdam), the border is wider, the edge not lobed, with hatching in *famille verte* style punctuated by cartouches in reserve with butterflies. All the pieces are decorated with very rich colours: blue, red, green, manganese, yellow, black.

87

87 Vase and dish: delftware, high-temperature polychrome, mid-18th century. Vase: H. 27.5 cm, dish: 23.3 cm. Musée des Arts décoratifs, Paris: inv. D. 23 370 and D. 23 415.

A large number of pieces in the mid-eighteenth century introduce a decoration intended to be Far Eastern, but with the sources only half-remembered. The motifs are distributed without any notion of the original idea, while a much more European kind of motif is used for the frame, giving the piece a naïve quality, not without charm. The dish has two amusing motifs: a 'perforated rock' placed on a spray of flowers typical of Japanese Imari ware, and, on the left, a very free interpretation of a Chinese symbol, which has lost all meaning

The baluster vase has exactly the same design conception, with identical framing motifs and the very same palette of colours.

88, 89 Two oval plaques: delftware, high-temperature polychrome, early 18th century. L. 43 cm, W. 38 cm. Private collection.

Among the most decorative pieces of delftware are these plaques with iridescent colours representing 'slender ladies' (*meiren*). The tradition certainly persisted for some time and the form varied. It has been suggested, without proof, that the earliest had a plain frame and that, following developments in taste, a few years later the rim was scalloped or foliated. The quality of the colour range and the richness of design are sufficient evidence that all these pieces belong to the 'golden age' of delftware production. The presence of black and pale mauve are proof of this. The mannerist style of the terrace that forms the base of the composition is to be noted, with the figures on it; 'perforated rocks' stand out in reserve on a blue ground. Another experiment inspired from China is in the drawing of the faces: red for the female figures, blue for the boy. It is to be deduced that these plaques were generally made in pairs to be placed on each side of a fireplace or a door.

88

89

90

90 Plate: delftware, high-temperature polychrome, c. 1720. D. 23 cm. Musée national Adrien Dubouché, Limoges: inv. 2 370, Gasnault Collection.

The theme of the vase of flowers was very often used by delftware painters. It is applied on a large number of rectangular or indented plaques, on plates and dishes. The circular outline of tableware makes it necessary to adapt the design to the form. Here the principal motif, skilfully arranged so that the bouquet occupies almost exactly half the space, is flanked by two little Chinamen sitting on each side: they fill very naturally what would otherwise be a blank space. The rim motifs, as is often the case, alternate in colour and reserve.

91 Lidded jar: delftware, high-temperature polychrome, mark W.K., c. 1700. H. 45 cm. Musée des Arts décoratifs, Paris: inv. 23 417.

This vase, one of a pair, has the classic form of a garniture piece. The decoration is a rather naïve rendering of the domestic scenes frequent on Chinese porcelains of the late Ming dynasty. It has round-faced Chinese ladies moving about in what is conceived as a Far Eastern interior and surrounded by leaves and water plants. On the lid is the dancing child very popular on the Japanese-style Chinese porcelain of the Kangxi period, imitated ad nauseam by the Delft potters.

92 93

92 Tea caddy: delftware, high-temperature polychrome on a black ground, c. 1700. H. 90 cm, W. 50 cm. Private collection.

This type of very small tea caddy is always rectangular in shape. The lid closes with a screw thread. The decoration looks as though it had been handled by a miniaturist. The ground has alternating green and blue stripes and, against it, the oval medallions in reserve contain quite simple plant motifs on a painted black ground. The medallions are placed on each of the four sides and on the lid, seeming to imitate lacquer painting.

93 Tea caddy: delftware, high-temperature polychrome on a black ground, Mark L.V.E. (Lambertus van Eenhoorn), c. 1700. H. 10 cm. Victoria and Albert Museum, London: inv. C. 2346 - 1910.

This little tea caddy, with its designs in golden yellow and green deriving from 'pagoda' landscapes, is very characteristic of Lambertus van Eenhoorn's manner of glazing in black. The colours are always applied thickly. The inside is glazed white.

Though black-glazed pieces are rather rare, quite a number of these small tea caddies are so treated (no more than 10 cm in height). They are real curios, always very carefully executed both in shaping and in their two-colour decoration. Some are not marked, but it can be surmised that they all come from the same factory.

94 Vase: delftware, high-temperature polychrome, c. 1710. D. 14 cm. ▶
Musée national de Céramique, Sèvres: inv. 9 921.

This vase is one of a pair and belongs to the garniture category; it certainly had a lid. This is a particularly striking example of Japanese influence from imported Imari ware. Leopard, spray, palisade, perched bird are seen with the 'perforated rock'. The shoulder has a strange treatment with coloured motifs against a ground of blue spirals. The palette includes a certain manganese-purple that is found on other pieces and seems to have been the speciality of one period or one factory.

95

95 Coffee-pot: delftware, high-temperature polychrome on a black ground, *c*. 1700. H. 26 cm. Stedelijk Museum 'Het Prinsenhof', Delft.

The variety of shapes for closed forms, especially coffee-pots, devised by the potters of Delft is quite extraordinary. This one, with its strict conical profile, its large handle and rectilinear spout, is rather unexpectedly reminiscent of the shape of certain Near Eastern ewers. The magnificent black glaze sets off the palette of blue, yellow, green and a very special kind of red. This is used for a very elegant design on the body consisting of the traditional plants and 'perforated rocks' with a heron standing by the waterside. There are notably strange motifs on the handle.

96 Plate: delftware, high-temperature ▶ polychrome, *c*. 1725. D. 26 cm. Musée national de Céramique, Sèvres: inv. 1 931.

Typical of one aspect of Sino-Japanese influence, the 'pagoda' motif at times takes on a very rich aspect. The conventional element tending towards 'chinoiserie' type of design is already present. Rather extravagant buildings are animated with figures, and there are flowering branches of the type found on Japanese Imari ware. On the left, a large patch of blue can be read as partly rock, partly cloud. The rim has the very frequent motifs of lambrequin scrolls, swags and pompoms. The painter has achieved great intensity of colour with his handling of the yellows and reds.

97

97 Figurine: delftware, high-temperature polychrome on a black ground, lst quarter of 18th century. H. 15.5 cm. Musées royaux d'Art et d'Histoire, Brussels: inv. 257, Evenepoël Collection.

This horse (one of a pair) clearly shows Far Eastern influence. The black glaze lends it a rather precious look. It is very similar to the one featuring a rider (cf. Pl. 162) and certainly comes from the same mould. The polychrome motifs in red, green, blue, yellow and white stand out amazingly on the black ground. Though unmarked, it can be assumed that it, too, comes from the Two Little Ships factory.

98 Plate: delftware, high-temperature polychrome on a black ground, c. 1710. D. 22 cm. Musée national de Céramique, Sèvres: inv. 21 927.

A black glaze over a brownish clay is painted in yellow and green with an overall Chinese landscape of remarkable quality. Behind 'perforated rocks' sketched in green in the foreground are pagodas, trees and fences with birds and insects flying among them. The sky streaked with cloud reveals the disk of the moon, reminding us that this is a night landscape, as the choice of the two colours confirms.

99

99 Teapot: delftware, high-temperature polychrome on an olive ground, mark L.V.D. (Lieven van Dalen), *c.* 1700. H. 80 cm, W. 10 cm. Private collection.

The colour of glaze called 'olive' is a quite particular one. Henry Havard first asserted that Lucas van Dalen was to be regarded as the inventor of the glaze. Later, it was discovered by C.H. de Jonge that it was in fact Lieven van Dalen, junior, who had bought back the Young Moor's Head factory from Rochus Jacobsz Hoppesteyn in 1692 and, therefore, invented the glaze. As Helbig indicates, Van Dalen resold his factory in 1727 a few years before his death.

This little teapot has the mark L.V.D. in yellow. The comparatively simple decoration consists of interlaced flowers with yellow stems, with some blue, white and red.

100 Oval plaque: delftware, high-temperature polychrome on a black ground, *c.* 1710. H. 32 cm, W. 27 cm. Musées royaux d'Art et d'Histoire, Brussels: inv. V. 526, Gustave Vermeersch Collection.

Plaques probably provided the best support for the painters who used black grounds to produce a precious effect, with quite unexpected pinks and a very lovely emerald green. One has a strong impression that the artist who decorated this piece combined several different elements that are not very homogeneous. The musician and dancing girl especially have little coherence with the tables laid with vases and the fence. The link is created by the flowering earth at the bottom of the plaque and by the magnificent phoenix (*fenghuang*) in gaudy colours at the top. The piped border is rather unusual in form, with oblique palmettes in green and yellow.

101 Vase: delftware, high-temperature yellow on a chocolate ground, *c.* 1710. H. 28 cm. Rijksmuseum, Amsterdam: inv. R.B.K. 1960 - 172.

The dark brown grounds called 'chocolate', with golden yellow decoration, are of as great an interest as the black and the 'olive' grounds. The superimposition of the yellow on the brown creates a sumptuous effect. A number of lidded garniture jars belonging to this category are known. Though without its lid, this vase is among the best examples for the quality of its glaze and the delicacy of the design, especially rich with its pagoda, fence, the abundance of floral motifs and the phoenix (*fenghuang*). The palmette frieze round the base and on the shoulder, the care given to the veining of the leaves and the elegant motifs on the neck are worth noting.

102

102 Two obelisks: delftware, Delft *doré*, mark L.V.E. (Lambertus van Eenhoorn), 1st quarter of 18th century. H. 18.5 cm. Musée des Beaux-Arts, Lille, Vicq Donation.

These little obelisks in the 'mixed technique' ware called Delft *doré* were presumably made as table ornaments. Each side has a different motif: 'beauties', Japanese children, pagodas, painted with great care. Many details show that they are not really a pair: the colouring of the knob, the shape and decoration of the feet, the borders of the plinths. The palette is blue, red, green and manganese-purple, with very discreet gilding. The mark L.V.E. in red is rather unusual on Delft *doré*.

103 Tulip vase and two bottles: delftware, Delft *doré,* mark under the ▶ tulip vase P.A.K. (Pieter Adriaensz Kocks). Tulip vase: H. 24 cm, W. 27 cm, bottles: H. 23 cm. Private collection.

Bulb bowls may take incredibly varied forms, but they all follow a few well-defined principles of style. Here the tulip vase has a heart-shaped body and rests on a pedestal, the five mouths are arranged in a fan, and the potter has added a touch of frivolity by making handles in the form of fantastic animal heads; the colour scheme accentuates the bizarre effect, with the salmon-pink tinted monsters contrasting with the rich but simple palette of Delft *doré*.

The bottles no doubt formed part of a small-scale garniture. The bird standing on a 'perforated rock' and the spray of flowers are typical of this kind of ware.

103

104

104 Lidded porringer: delftware, Delft *doré,* mark P.A.K. (Pieter Adriaensz Kocks), early 18th century. D. 12 cm. Gemeente Museum, The Hague: inv. OCD. 3.1971.

This porringer, or small tureen, has an unusual shape, with a raised scalloped rim into which the lid fits well down. The square handles are an attempt to imitate Far Eastern forms. The Japanese motifs typical of Imari ware, a clog-shaped junk, a 'perforated rock' and flowering shrubs, are of rare fidelity. The whole effect is a combination of great delicacy of execution with a bold liberty of interpretation, making it an outstanding piece.

105 Ewer: delftware, Delft *doré,* mark P.A.K. (Pieter Adriaensz Kocks), 2nd quarter of 18th century. H. 25 cm. Musée national Adrien Dubouché, Limoges: inv. 1 025, Gasnault Collection.

This 'helmet' ewer was a type commonly found at Rouen and also at Delft. It comes from the metalwork of the time of Louis XIV. At Delft it is often fluted, as here. Instead of showing classical motifs, such as are usually found on French faience, this draws on the East but with a rather rare fantasy: the little dancer next to the 'beauty' or 'slender lady' is not unrelated to the *Commedia dell'arte*. The palette is very rich. Note, too, the fanciful bird placed beside the little figure. The design is repeated on both sides of the vessel. It is interesting that a basin accompanied this ewer and that the 'Het Princessehof' Museum in Leeuwarden has an example showing exactly the same decoration, illustrated by De Jonge in *Delft Ceramics,* Pl. 258.

105

106 107

106   Plate: delftware, Delft *doré*, mark W.K., 1st quarter of 18th century. D. 22 cm. Musée national de Céramique, Sèvres: inv. 5 822 (1), Petitet Donation.

The major part of Delft *doré* is devoted to representations of Sino-Japanese scenes. It may be that the different factories interpreted them in different ways. The decorator with the monogram W.K. here provides a rich interpretation of two 'beauties' and a parrot, in a setting that divides the composition vertically, on one side a curtained building, on the other the habitual vase of flowers. The asymmetry is stressed by the strangely jagged line of the ground on the right.

107   Bowl: delftware, Delft *doré*, mark A.R., 1st quarter of 18th century. D. 19 cm. Musée des Beaux-Arts, Lille, Van der Straten Donation.

The Musée des Beaux-Arts at Lille has a pair of bowls as strange in their shape as in their decoration. They are good evidence of the amazing variety of the potter who signed himself A.R. The embossed shape is remote from Oriental forms. The decoration must certainly refer to the sun: a human face in the middle of the well of the bowl, from which radiate rays conceived according to a very old tradition with alternating triangles and flames. This must have been influenced by the 'sun of St Bernardin', appearing in European decorative art ever since the Renaissance. The general impression is of the metal ornaments, appliqués and facings widespread in the period of Louis XIV.

108   Polygonal dish: delftware, Delft *doré*, 1st quarter of 18th century. ▶ D. 34 cm. Musée national de Céramique, Sèvres: inv. 3 541.

Some of the most faithful reproductions of Far Eastern porcelain were pieces like this dish, imitating the Japanese Imari ware that had become so successful that it was even imitated in China. Delft gave great care to its interpretation. The flower vase on a tripod, the little landscapes in panels, where the blue has great intensity, are all designed to counterfeit porcelains. It is interesting to note that the Meissen porcelain factory also reproduced this type of dish about 1725. This 'brocaded Imari' type is also found in English porcelain.

109

109 Three plates: delftware, Delft *doré,* mark P.A.K. (Pieter Adriaensz Kocks), 1st quarter of 18th century. D. 22 cm. Musée national de Céramique, Sèvres: Centre: inv. 15 672, Moulard Donation, Left: inv. 16 447, Papillon Bequest, Right: inv. 3 316.

Services for the various courts of Europe were doubtless made to compete with the armorial wares of the Dutch East India Company.
  Centre: This plate with the arms of Nicolas Auguste de la Baume, Marshal of France in 1703, chevalier du Saint Esprit in 1705, died on 22 October 1716, provides us with a precise range of dates stretching over 11 years, derived from the emblems on it. The rim has a very special design based on Chinese Kangxi-period motifs, often called 'Chinese Imari'.
  Left: More than one piece survives from the service with the arms of Frederick I, king of Prussia from 1701 to 1713. He was also the Elector of Brandenburg, hence the alternating black and red eagles that form the main feature of the rim with the crowned FR (Fredericus Rex) monogram.
  Right: Another well-known example of armorial services is that of Louis Alexandre de Bourbon, count of Toulouse, the third legitimized son of Louis XIV and Madame de Montespan. He was born in 1678, was Admiral of France from 1683 at the age of five and died in 1737. The rim has alternating fleur-de-lis and fleurons. The wreath around the cavetto is the same on the plate of Frederick I and that of the count.

110 Plate: delftware, Delft *doré,* mark P.A.K. (Pieter Adriaensz Kocks). 1st quarter of 18th century. D. 22 cm. Private collection.

This Delft *doré* service with the royal arms of England is very well known. The arms are those compiled after 1714. The order was certainly accompanied by precise drawings as all the heraldic charges and bearings figure in the composition. In contrast to the majority of armorial pieces, the rim is decorated with very simple fleurons. The palette is very rich: turquoise blue, grey and green in addition to blue, red and gold.

111 Plate: delftware, polychrome enamels, mark W.K., *c.* 1720. D. 22.5 cm. Private collection.

The design on this plate is known as the 'flower vase' (*au vase fleuri*). It comes from a known pricked drawing that is more often executed in the 'mixed technique' of Delft *doré,* when the lambrequin motif of the rim includes high-fired blue. Here it is all done in enamels, with a dominant light red, green and some gold. The only difference is the absence of blue, and the two styles of production may thus be considered contemporary. Furthermore, the piece bears the unexplained monogram, W.K., in red, while the pieces in 'mixed technique' generally have the monogram P.A.K.

114

110

111

112

112 Dish: delftware, Delft *doré,* mark P.A.K. (Pieter Adriaensz Kocks), 1st quarter of 18th century. D. 40 cm. Rijksmuseum, Amsterdam: inv. 409, Loudon Collection.

This dish is something rather exceptional in the Delft *doré* technique. Unlike most pieces in this ware, the decoration is European in style. Not only the subject treated in the centre, *The Rape of Europa,* is taken from an engraving by Hendrik Goltzius, but the rich frame follows the fashion of European ornament, in which perhaps can be detected motifs dear to Daniel Marot. There are shells, a latticed braid, scrolls and volutes, some of which are picked out in reserve on the high-temperature blue ground. Some find this piece in questionable taste, but the very fine palette, including red, blue, emerald green, yellow, black, pink, mauve, grey, with the gold playing among them, is certainly a tour de force on the part of the painter. Should we regard this as a work intended as an examination, or master, piece by a faience potter, which would explain the trouble he has taken with his signature, written with particular care?

113 Lidded vase: delftware, polychrome enamels, *c.* 1760. H. 33 cm. ▶
Musée national de Céramique, Sèvres: inv. 1 931(7).

Both in shape and decoration this type of vase is as close an imitation as possible of a Chinese *famille rose* model. The shape is a very slender baluster, with the lid greatly overhanging the neck. The palette is very individual, consisting, besides gold, of light blue, two greens, an iron red, a lilac, a yellow and a brown: the painter was much concerned to treat the flowers in a wide variety of polychrome colours. The shoulder decoration is very elaborate and testifies to the difficulties of execution, because the pigments were all very thick.

This piece entered the Musée national de Céramique in 1835 and was bought at The Hague. A very old label stuck on the piece notes that it is similar in every point to a vase in a collection in Lille, which has in the guise of a mark: *Sophia de Nane.* A family de Nane is known at Delft, notably at the Roman factory.

113

114

115

114 Spittoon with handle: delftware, enamels and gilt, c. 1750. H. 18 cm. Rijksmuseum, Amsterdam: inv. N.M. 12 400 - 403.

This shape, as can be seen elsewhere, belongs among the accessories of the smoking-room. The globular body with a handle is surmounted by a broad flaring rim. The decoration is amusingly close to that on the cylindrical tobacco jar (Pl. 138). Both 'colonial' and European figures are portrayed smoking their pipes, along with Blacks who are occupied with the preparation of the tobacco. The very delicate decoration for such a prosaic object includes charming butterfly motifs round the underside of the rim.

115 Plate: delftware, polychrome enamels, 2nd quarter of 18th century. D. 22.8 cm. Musée des Arts décoratifs, Paris: inv. D. 22 314.

Scenes from the life of Christ, especially the Crucifixion, were used very frequently as a subject for both high-temperature and enamelled wares. Strangely enough, they nearly always recall very closely the 'Jesuit ware' porcelains of the East India Company, produced in Jesuit-run factories in China and decorated with Christian saints; the decorations were done either in polychrome or grisaille. The Far Eastern contribution is even more assertive in the rim decoration, where we see motifs inspired from the Chinese 'Eight Precious Objects' depicted in cartouches in reserve on a floral ground. Red dominates to an almost aggressive extent in the palette, which also contains green, blue and yellow.

116 Dish: delftware, polychrome enamels, mark A.R. (Ary van Rijsselberg), 1st half of 18th century. D. 30 cm. Rijksmuseum, Amsterdam: inv. 12 400 - 362, Loudon Collection.

In Japanese style, this obviously humorous motif done in enamels is quite common. It looks as though the inspiration was taken from a print, and, without harming the quality of the decoration, was given a sense of caricature. The very delicate frieze round the rim is composed of a trellis and fleurons. The palette consists of only three kinds of red, a blue and a green, with great richness of effect. The gold is so skilfully applied that it adds great gaiety to the whole. On the back, stylized fleurons in red accompany the mark. Several pieces of this type are known, dishes and plates, so that probably it was once all one service.

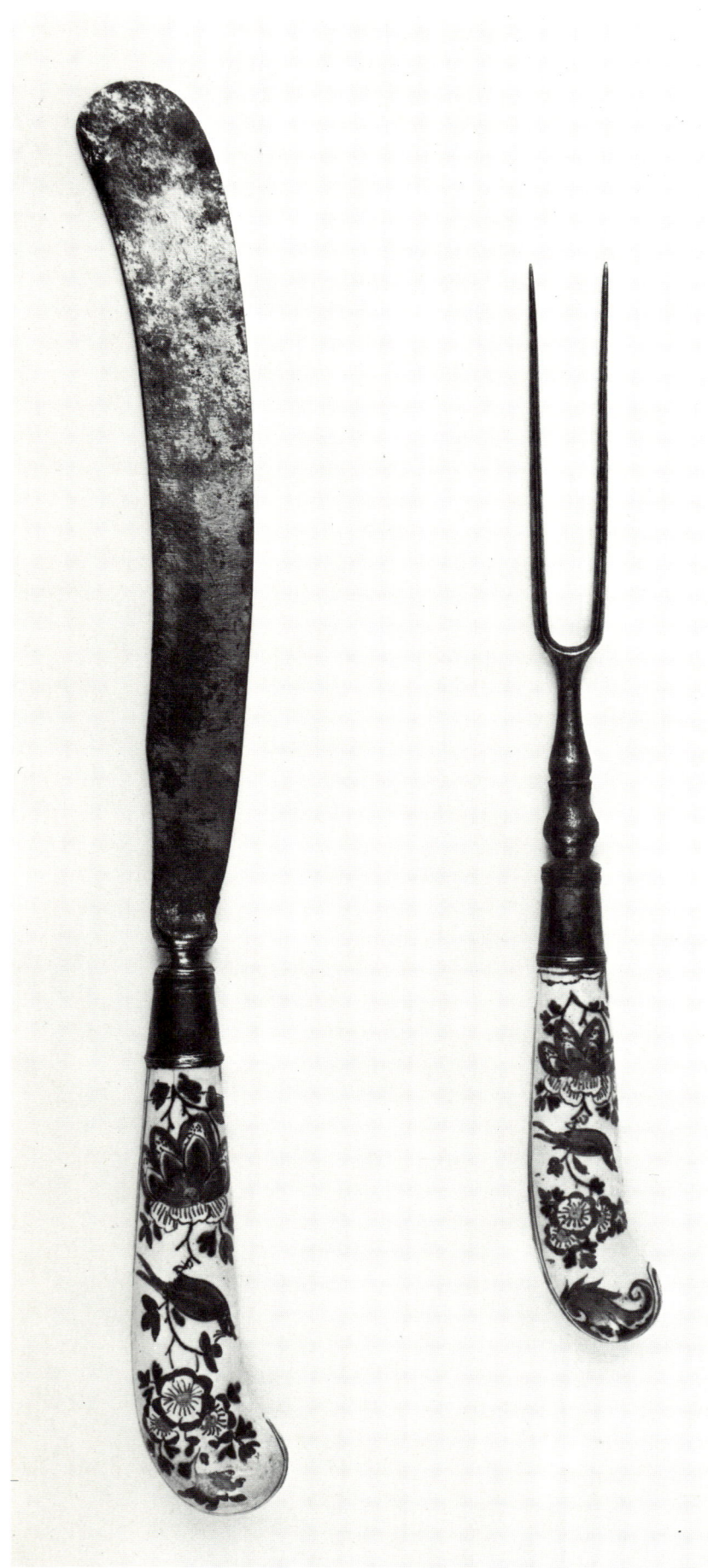

118

117 Knife and fork: delftware, Delft *doré, c.* 1730. Knife: L. 27.2 cm. fork: L. 20.5 cm. Musée des Arts décoratifs, Paris: inv. 27 629 A and 27 629 B.

Knife and fork handles of faience and porcelain became quite popular in the early eighteenth century. The Dutch East India Company produced large numbers, as did many European factories, but these handles in Delft *doré* with the classic perching bird motif seem rather to be imitations of Far Eastern pieces. The shape, curved at the end, is found frequently and is often on similar objects in European porcelain, especially in French soft-paste porcelain and at Meissen.

118 Globe: delftware, blue-and-white, mark L.V.E. (Lambertus van Eenhoorn), early 18th century. H. 12 cm. Musée national de Céramique, Sèvres: inv. 19 193.

Several pieces of this curious type are known with a globe in its chest; they were made as ornaments for the work table. The theme of the motifs is trade and navigation, and the panels contain symbolic female figures: here Justice and Abundance. They are treated with great vitality and emphasized by vigorous dark outlining (*trek*). A hole at the top makes it possible that the piece was made as a pen-holder.

117

VI THE EVOLUTION OF STYLES AND SHAPES DURING THE EIGHTEENTH CENTURY

It is often said that after the first quarter of the eighteenth century delftware began to lose its aristocratic character and that the competition of foreign faience (and then of foreign porcelain) drove the shareholders (*winkelhouders*) to go after a new clientele, with less exacting tastes and smaller financial resources. This hypothesis is only a half-truth. We can follow a progressive transformation that does not always fit this generalization.

BLUE-AND-WHITE WARE

Pl. 120 In this technique a return to European subjects is manifest to some degree. We still find landscapes taken from contemporary engravings, seascapes and religious subjects.

Pl. 119 To this period belong the sets of plates (generally twelve in number) reproducing series of prints. The best known are the 'months of the year', each illustrated by its labour in the fields and often accompanied by the appropriate sign of the Zodiac in a medallion. There are also scenes of fishing in the far north. One of the latter

Pl. 121 series is taken from the paintings of Van der Meulen, giving us the 'Herring Fishery', the 'Whale Hunt' and the 'Sea Hunt'. The notion of reproducing portraits con-

Pl. 68 tinued: figures of monarchs and even of painters are found on ornamental plaques as well as on dishes.

HIGH-TEMPERATURE POLYCHROME PAINTING

This remained as important as ever and of as high a quality. Various types (which must have been very successful, given the number of examples surviving) are dated to

Pl. 122 this period. Among these is the 'lightning' (*bliksem dekor*) pattern of Japanese inspiration: on a ground resembling clouds, a water plant in an irregular panel stands out in reserve. Zigzag bands come out from this central motif, hence its name. In fact, the bands represent the little footbridges of Japanese gardens, and the central motif is the water sign; pieces occasionally have only the central motif. Some writers think that the motif appeared earlier than is usually thought. Like the 'heart' motif discussed below, the water sign certainly spread to every factory, for numerous marks are to be found associated with it.

Another equally common theme is the 'heart' motif. Pls. 124, 126 This gives scope for painting in reserve on a coloured ground, in green or more rarely in yellow. The design consists of arranging panels of lotus-leaf shape over the Pl. 123 ground, alternating with a kind of 'bud' from the same plant. Sometimes this motif can be found in other decorative arrangements.

Just as widespread is a composition consisting of very lush vegetation, characterized by the sort of clouds that symbolize water in China. Along with these well-known patterns, we must mention what is sometimes called the 'sampler' design, based on the Chinese arrangements of Pl. 127 'precious' or 'useful' objects, with various heterogeneous objects scattered over a white or coloured ground.

The 'basket of flowers' motif was never forsaken but gradually lost its Oriental stylization and became more naturalistic. Another model, much reproduced, which can be found throughout the life of the ware, is the 'peacock-feather' pattern with the feathers arranged like a fan in a vase; stylized flowers complete the design. This pattern was often very crudely handled.

FACTORY MARKS

An important event for historians of ceramics occurred about the middle of the eighteenth century. Several factories already in existence registered their marks and put them on most of their wares, so that from then on they are easily recognized. The Peacock factory did this about 1740, the Three Bells factory from 1750 to 1778 (with Van der Does), the Porcelain Claw factory about 1763 (with Lambertus Sanderus) and the White Star factory, from 1761 to 1772 (with Albertus Kiell, whose monogram, A.K., has sometimes led to confusion, although it is surmounted by a star). The Axe factory was certainly one of the most productive in the second half of the eighteenth century, but it had started marking its wares earlier, in about 1739 (with Justus Brouwer).

THE INFLUENCE OF EUROPEAN FAIENCE AND PORCELAIN

Although, as we have seen, direct Far Eastern influence continued without interruption until the end of the eighteenth century, various elements from European faience and porcelain production made themselves felt at dates not always easy to decide. This new influence was manifest in various guises, either in the choice of subjects or in the colours utilized. French iconography provided pastoral scenes, wrongly called *à la Watteau*, and even decorative motifs.

It is the coloured grounds, however, that show the greatest effects of this influence. These are coloured glazes, not to be confused with the painted grounds referred to earlier, particularly in connection with the 'heart' motif. These coloured grounds are of several kinds. After the specifically Dutch black and chocolate grounds, blue grounds appeared. These have naturally been likened to Nevers ware. They vary from rather deep blue that might be mistaken for Nevers ware to a rather pale hue more comparable to ware from Rouen. In some cases the design is applied in opaque white as at Nevers; in others, a modicum of polychrome painting is permitted.

At a later date, pieces with yellow glaze appear, reminiscent of a well-known southern European type of ware, but their floral decoration is usually quite unrelated to French wares with yellow grounds.

Another type of coloured ground is perhaps more attractive: the not very common turquoise. This may indicate the influence of certain European porcelains but it must be allowed that the motifs (often very 'Japanese') are quite unlike any of the decorations on turquoise from Meissen or Sèvres.

Another uncommon type of ground belongs to a tradition which began in Italy, then passed through northern France and Scandinavia and became quite common in England. It uses a glaze tinted with grey-blue as a ground for decoration in opaque white and drawing in manganese-purple. Several pieces of this type have the 'Fortune' mark. These Dutch pieces certainly come closest to English ware. Ware with so-called 'chestnut' grounds on which flowers and leaves stand out in reserve, resembling the French style, is of quite inferior quality.

A rather special, very elegant ware is dated to about 1760. It consists of a coloured ground (sometimes even black) with floral decoration, often chrysanthemums, in which irregular panels are left in reserve. These panels contain charming little Chinese or European scenes. One type of trompe-l'œil decoration, found on much European faience, was also produced at Delft: the 'playing card' motifs, so densely painted that the ground is invisible.

ENAMELLED WARE

The use of the muffle kiln continued in the second half of the eighteenth century, but often for other purposes. Influenced by European porcelain, a new type of decoration that betrays the influence of Meissen began in about 1750, with nothing Oriental about it. There are genre scenes, set in rococo frames, and floral scatters, all painted in detail. The shapes are generally porringers, butter dishes, little boxes, water cisterns (perhaps more Dutch in style) and ornamental plaques with pastoral subjects after Van Berghem.

Henry Havard's theory that it was the appearance of enamel (*petit feu*) decoration that hastened the decline of the art of faience at Delft is no longer accepted. On the contrary, it would seem that this much more costly technique aimed at competing with foreign wares and especially with porcelain. It was rather, as Hudig says, the country's economic difficulties that brought about the gradual disappearance of these methods by around 1765.

SHAPES

Shapes diversified during the eighteenth century. In the service pieces it is worth remembering that, starting from about 1750, dishes and plates often were no longer thin; they adopted the usual profile of the period. Butter dishes became more and more common and took forms strange enough to bring them into the category of trompe-l'œil. Influenced by products from rival foreign factories, tureens appeared, especially oval ones. Some had feet, some had convoluted handles borrowed from metalwork; others were less rococo but still ribbed or reeded with a knob simulating some plant form.

A kettle on a tripod stand became popular and called for much virtuosity on the part of the potter. Similar is the coffee-pot on feet, in a very rococo style, which poured through a tap fixed in the mouth of a mascaron. Lighting fixtures were the pretext for many extravagant compositions framed in foliage and flowers in quasi-naturalist style. Candlesticks sometimes even took the form of a branch. Then, too, there were fruit baskets (some supported by faces), cream jugs, porringers, bowls, jam pots, wine-glass coolers with feet and masks.

Garniture sets continued to be made, often with differently shaped vases: facets with rococo motifs (sometimes in relief) framing little panels generally indicate a late-eighteenth-century date. Many water cisterns resemble French and German faience, and puzzle jugs in Rouen style became common. Barbers' bowls, as well as curious sledge-shaped vessels, were made both in high-temperature ware and in enamels.

Rijsttafelstel or sweetmeat dishes, like that preserved in the Stedelijk Museum 'Het Prinsenhof' at Delft, are also dated to about 1750.

The taste expressed by the new clientele of this period often gave rise to curiously shaped creations of varying felicity, many of them in the trompe-l'œil technique, which will be studied separately. These inventions are more often proof of the potter's virtuosity than of his taste. For example, vases shaped like sledges are well known and were extremely popular. They must go back quite early, since some enamelled ones are known.

Another extraordinary object is the bird cage. It may be round, square or oblong. The upper part is a dome; perforated bars provide for the fixing of metal rods; a seed box is arranged as a drawer at the bottom. These cages must have had some success, because they were manufactured at Lille too. They were generally made to be suspended.

Some flower vases were even more fantastic, for instance busts with Oriental faces, where the tops of the heads are pierced to hold flowers. The influence of porcelain can often be seen: vases and ewers were frequently decorated in relief with 'lettuce' or 'celery' leaves in the Sèvres manner.

The manufacture of pharmacists' jars was considerable. Hudig has pointed out that the syrup jar (*siroop kan*) figures in the guild's regulations as early as 1654 as a test piece for faience throwers qualifying as masters. We have to realize, therefore, that drug jars formed part of the repertory of Delft potters from an early date. However, though they may have been frequent in the time of Dutch majolica manufacture, we are forced to recognize that nearly all the drug jars known to us date from the late eighteenth and even the early nineteenth century.

Their forms include an albarello and a cylindrical ointment jar, sometimes a larger vase of the same shape and, lastly, perhaps the most interesting, the pear-shaped syrup jars with a handle and very short spout, resting on a ringed foot. The foot is generally flat, with or without a moulded joint, but some pieces have a kind of bell, often quite high, which makes us think the size of the vase allowed the jar to be placed in warm water to melt a syrup that had become too thick.

The decoration of these vessels has little variety. There is a frame for the inscription panel with cherubs and peacocks (sometimes fish) on high-temperature faience. Delft, of course, was not the only place where such jars were made; very similar ones come from the English factory at Lambeth, just outside London, from Brussels, from Lille, etc. Enamelled drug jars (albarelli and ointment jars) are generally decorated with the figure of a stag.

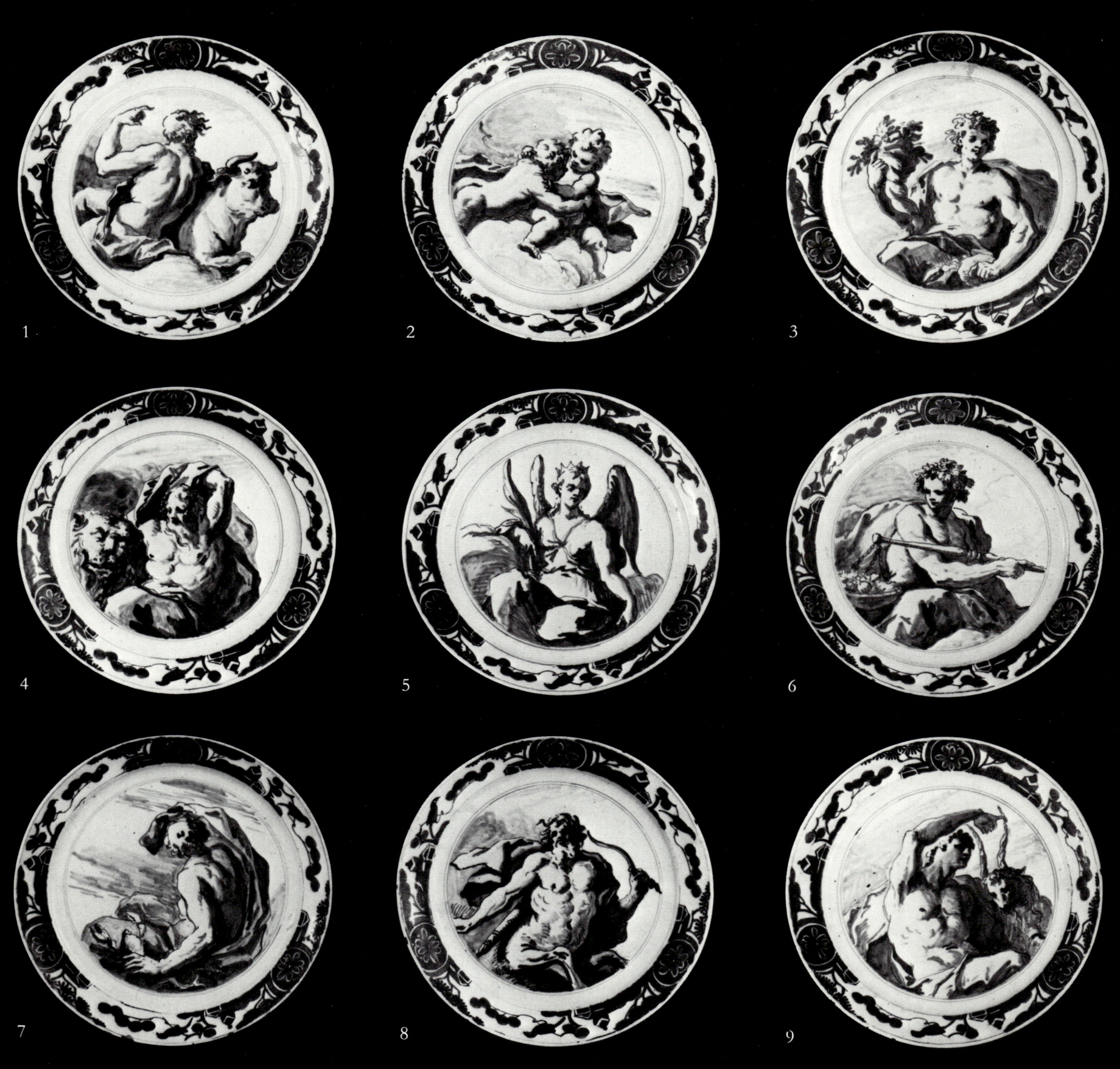

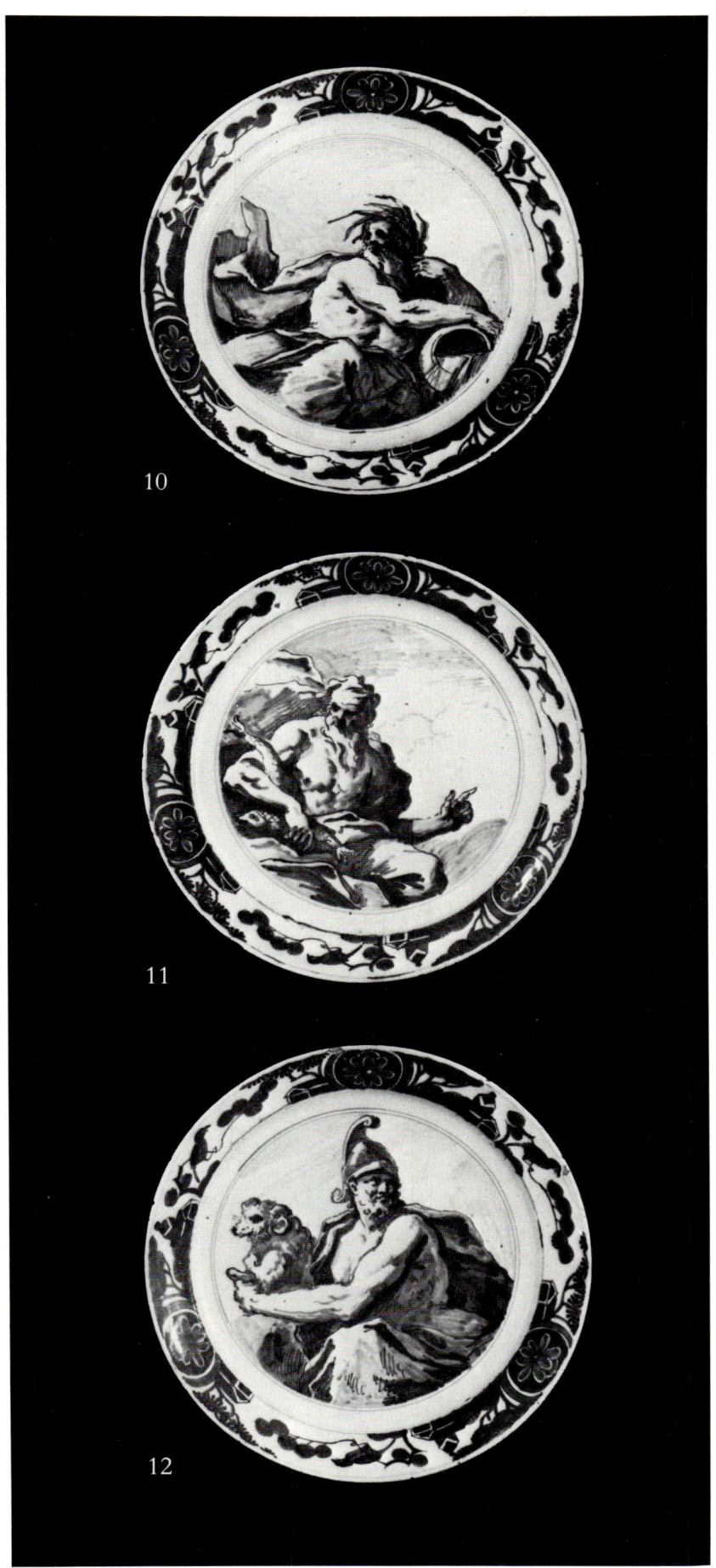

119 Set of twelve plates: delftware, blue-and-white, dated 1711. D. 20.3. cm. British Museum, London: inv. P.S. 04-73-47.

This famous service marks a very interesting point in the history of delftware. Each plate bears a sign of the zodiac. 1: The Bull (Taurus); 2: The Twins (Gemini); 3: The Crab (Cancer); 4: The Lion (Leo); 5: The Virgin (Virgo); 6: The Scales (Libra); 7: The Scorpion (Scorpio); 8: The Archer (Saggitarius); 9: The Goat (Capricornus); 10: The Water-carrier (Aquarius); 11: The Fish (Pisces); 12: The Ram (Aries). The back of each piece is signed *J. Thornhill fecit. Delph Aug : 1711*. The plates have traditionally been thought of as actually painted by the English artist Sir James Thornhill, Queen Ann's historical painter at the time, and were in the possession of his daughter Mary who married Hogarth. This hypothesis has been corroborated by the fact that the word *Delph* was the English name for Delft. We side with several other authorities, however, in believing that the painter Thornhill supplied drawings to a Delft potter, who copied them faithfully. The fidelity is striking. The painter specialized in architectural decoration, and the representations of the signs of the zodiac are interpreted very broadly, in the manner of this kind of painting. It is rather interesting that the framing of these figures—the same on each plate—is in the usual style of current wares, and of Far Eastern inspiration.

120

120 Water jug: delftware, blue-and-white, mark I. BAAN, dated 1760. H. 21 cm. Musée national de Céramique, Sèvres: inv. 6 014.

This flat-handled jug is a marriage piece, as is shown by the inscriptions. On the front we read *D: yonge Cornelis* in a large cartouche; on the right: *Flora Bax;* while on each side of a mill are inscribed *Hoog* and *Moët*; below a fishing vessel is written *Heyme Versteegh*. Along the top are three cherub heads; on the handle is a fish and the date 1760. This type of piece is often called folk ware; it is interesting in its implications of a changing clientele in the second half of the eighteenth century.

121 Five plates: delftware, blue-and-white, mark an axe (Porcelain Axe factory), 2nd half of 18th century. D. 22.5 cm. Musée Carnavalet, Paris, Liesville Collection: inv. 1-4,6.

It appears that quite early the potters at Delft thought of decorating whole series of pieces on a given theme. The Rose factory, for instance, made a series of scenes from the Gospels, and the series illustrating the 'Months of the Year' is well known. In the second half of the eighteenth century some factories, notably Justus Arouwer's Porcelain Axe factory, produced scenes such as 'Whale Hunting' or 'Herring Fishing'. Generally, as here, the subject is in colour, and many of the engravings used are recognizably by great masters such as Van der Meulen. The title of the scene is written in a reserve cartouche and preceded by a number.

126

122 Plate: delftware, high-temperature polychrome, mark D.P.A.W. (Peacock factory), early 18th century. D. 23 cm. Musée national de Céramique, Sèvres: inv. 1 267.

One of the best known designs among the polychrome decoration of Delft is that called 'lightning' motif or *bliksem dekor*, wrongly attributing the zigzags adorning these pieces, which seem to emerge from a cloud. In fact, the irregular outline in the centre of the piece that forms a frame for a cluster of water plants seems to be a reminiscence of the Far Eastern 'water sign', while the zigzags fencing the flowers of the background recall the little bridges of Japanese gardens. The three motifs of spheres straddling the rim and wall are more difficult to identify. This design was long used unaltered. De Jonge, on the basis of a piece preserved in the Gemeente Museum, Arnhem, marked W.K. for Willem Cleffius, dates the beginnings of this type as early as the late seventeenth century. Many pieces are not marked or, like this one, bear the later mark of the Peacock factory. The plate at the Gemeente Museum, Arnhem, has a slightly indented rim, whereas the majority of pieces have smooth, round rims.

122

123 Plate: delftware, high-temperature polychrome, mark K.V.D.K., dated 1736. D. 22.5 cm. Musée des Arts décoratifs, Paris: inv. 23 388.

124 Dish: delftware, high-temperature polychrome, 1st half of 18th century. D. 35 cm. Private collection.

It is interesting to see how different painters alter a given decorative system. The 'hearts' on this plate, enclosing Far Eastern flowers and landscapes, are painted in reserve on a decorated ground that is here in quite another style, as though an attempt were being made to renovate the genre. Instead of straight bands joining the water-lily-shaped cartouches, we have a curved braid; round it are motifs reminiscent of the famous Chinese *ruyi* sceptre. All the floral and plant motifs are in reserve on the blue ground. They are painted in red with a few touches of green. The mark K.V.D.K. with the date is not identified. There is a piece of blue-and-white in the Musée national de Céramique, Sèvres, with the mark K.V.K. and the date 1731.

Though widespread, the 'heart' motif is very rarely mentioned by earlier writers, for some unexplained reason. The 'heart' is in fact a misnomer and derives from a decorative effect of Japanese inspiration: cartouches in the form of water-lily leaves. The 'heart' motif on a yellow ground is much rarer than on a green one. The presence of this yellow gives an unusual richness to the decorative effect. Instead of the blue lines over the ground, there are red curves behaving as a complementary colour. Several of these pieces show the mongram I.V.L. on the back, attributed to Jansz van der Laan, but we see a discrepancy in dating here.

A warning should be given of the existence of nineteenth- and twentieth-century imitations of this type.

124

125

125 Dish and vase: delftware, high-temperature polychrome, the dish with mark of a star (White Star factory); the vase with mark L.V.E. (Lambertus van Eenhoorn), early 18th century. Dish: D. 26 cm, vase: H. 25 cm, W. 20 cm. Musée national de Céramique, Sèvres: inv. 8 143 and 21 534.

Of Far Eastern motifs, the most frequent at Delft include water amid abundant vegetation. The two pieces illustrated here, though they bear different marks, are very close in their inspiration, and the palette itself is comparable. This form of two-handled vase is unusual. The key-fret motif round the neck is also found on Chinese ceramics. A comparison of these two pieces with the *rijsttafelstel* illustrated in Plate 57 confirms the hypothesis of Jean Helbig in his catalogue: with the vase marked L.V.E., classed in the first part of the eighteenth century, there is every likelihood that the two other pieces bearing the Star mark (White Star) are contemporary. He writes: 'The Star mark is certainly to be attributed to the *De Witte Starre* factory when it is accompanied by the initials of Albertus Kiell or Cornelis van den Bergh from 1761 to 1803. It seems logical however that the Star by itself, frequently used on quality pieces, also belongs to the same factory, for it would be curious if it had not marked its products during the whole of the first half of the eighteenth century....'

126 Jug and plate: delftware, high-temperature polychrome, mark A.R., early 18th century. Jug: H. 23 cm, plate: D. 22.5 cm. Musée national de Céramique, Sèvres: inv. 10 420 (jug), Grémiou Donation; inv. 3 711, (plate), Boucher de Perthes Donation.

In this example of the 'heart' motif, the ground is coloured green and enlivened by lines of blue, against which stand out shields in reserve in the shape of water-lily leaves; pine cones alternate with leaves, to which they are linked by a kind of blue braid. A rosette occupies the centre. The palette is limited to one green, one blue and one red. In spite of the simplicity of the motifs occupying the medallions and the slender range of colours, the decorative effect must have been very popular, for a large number of pieces exists at the present time, with many different factory marks. The distribution of the design is highly simplified on the jug because of the vessel's shape.

127

127 Plate: delftware, high-temperature polychrome, 2nd quarter of 18th century. D. 26.5 cm. Musée des Arts décoratifs, Paris: inv. D. 23 316.

One of the most widespread designs in the second quarter of the eighteenth century used by various European factories (Rouen and Sinceny especially) is a group of disparate objects based on the 'Eight Precious Objects' as interpreted on Chinese porcelain of the Kangxi period, with a scatter of vases, boxes, tables, brush-holders and teapots arranged according to the whim of the painter. There are always ribbons floating from most of the objects. The prototype is generally in blue-and-white, but Delft and Rouen both appear to have preferred to make these motifs a pretext for polychrome effects.

128 Plate: delftware, high-temperature polychrome, c. 1770. D. 22 cm. Musée national de Céramique, Sèvres: inv. 5 587.

Under a variety of influences, the shapes of dishes and plates changed in the late eighteenth century and became similar to those used in French factories. The decorative composition complied with the change in shape and adopted a well-defined frame. A number of pieces have motifs in the centre that still retain some reminiscence of Far Eastern influence: a palisade, a flowering branch, etc, but arranged in quite a different manner. The deer, shown here in an imaginary landscape, is like one preserved in a private collection and signed by one of the best faience potters of this period: Dextra.

128

129 Plaque with indented outline: delftware, high-temperature polychrome, c. 1750. H. 40 cm, W. 30 cm. Rijksmuseum, Amsterdam: inv. 12 400-133, Loudon Collection.

Among the wares that maintained a certain standard of quality for a long time during the eighteenth century are the plaques and dishes with gallant or pastoral scenes *à la française*. Like a print, this blue-and-white plaque is framed in polychrome by primarily rococo elements and is a fine example of its type. The black carnations, scrolls in reserve on a beautiful red ground and yellow roses are proof of the very great skill maintained by some producers of high-temperature faience well into the eighteenth century. Numerous pieces in the same spirit have come to light, the aim being to employ colours in accordance with old Delft traditions.

129

135

130

130 Puzzle jug (*Fop Kan*): delftware, blue-and-white, mark G.V.S. (Geertruy Verstelle), 2nd half of 18th century. H. 21.5 cm. Musée national de Céramique, Sèvres: inv. CL 7 475.

131 Jug: delftware, high-temperature decoration on a coloured ground, ▶ mark DAW (Peacock factory), *c.* 1720. H. 20 cm. Musée national de Céramique, Sèvres: inv. 5 801.

This very common form in French pottery was copied by the Chinese for the East India Company. The date it was adopted by the delftware potters is difficult to decide. The idea of the puzzle jug is that the perforated neck of the jug prevents the liquid inside it from being poured by tilting it. A channel runs through the handle and round the top of the neck; drinking is possible only by sucking through one of the three nozzles set round the mouth. All this requires great virtuosity on the part of the potter, and there is reason to believe that pots like this were made for passing a master's qualifying examination. The decoration, rococo floral frames and scenes of gallantry, clearly reflect the period of French influence. Geertruy Verstelle worked in the Old Moor's Head factory.

The dark blue ground typical of certain types of Nevers production from the seventeenth century on was imitated at Delft from a date not easy to determine. The jug (*kannetje*), in a typically Dutch shape, has a glaze of the colour termed 'Persian blue'. As often at Nevers, the design stands out in fixed white. It consists of a very freely handled floral decoration. The period of this production may be decided from a comparison with other marked pieces. A very similar jug in the Musées royaux d'Art et d'Histoire, Brussels, bears the mark DAW, known as that of the Peacock factory in the first half of the eighteenth century.

131

132

132 Money box: delftware, blue-and-white, Mark D.L.V., dated 1775, H. 28.5. cm. Musée des Arts décoratifs, Paris: inv. D. 23 345.

This kind of money box, of which there several examples, is in the shape of a baluster vase or goblet with a lid. The style of decoration is often European: scrolls, acanthus and naturalistic flowers are arranged in bands, and the vessel has a series of pastoral figures in a very simplified landscape. The upper part, in one with the body, has an oblique slit, here more carefully cut than on many other specimens where it cuts clumsily across the motif. The figure on the knob has touches of yellow and manganese. The initials D.L.V. with the date, 1775, are no more decipherable than the letters M.V.B., inscribed with the date, 1757, on a money box in the Musées royaux d'Art et d'Histoire, Brussels. Are they not perhaps the initials of the owner?

133 Strawberry bowl and its tray: delftware, high-temperature polychrome on a coloured ground, mark Van Duyn (Johannes van Duyn), c. 1770. Bowl: L. 25 cm, tray: L. 27.7 cm. Musées royaux d'Art et d'Histoire, Brussels: inv. 538 a and b, Evenepoël Collection.

Some writers think these two superposed dishes, one perforated, were for serving strawberries. The form is not typically Dutch. The yellow ground resembles southern French faiences, as does the polychrome floral decoration. Most of the pieces from Delft with yellow grounds have decoration analogous to this. This piece is signed by Johannes van Duyn, owner of the Porcelain Dish factory; he registered his mark in 1764.

133

134 Plate: delftware, high-temperature tinted ground, mark Fortuin (Fortune factory), 2nd half of 18th century. D. 26 cm. Musée national de Céramique, Sèvres: inv. 18 352, Chompret Bequest.

Decoration such as this, with a design in dark blue, manganese-purple and opaque white on a ground slightly tinted pale blue, seems only to have appeared relatively late at Delft, and mainly in the Fortune factory. The origins of it are Italian 'white on white' (*bianco sopra bianco*) ware; then it was taken up by certain faience factories in the north of France (Saint Amand les Eaux) and England (Bristol). Even the shape is no longer in the Dutch tradition. The stencil of this floral motif must have been used for a whole service because several similar examples are known.

135 Plate: delftware, high-temperature polychrome, *c.* 1750. D. 23.3 cm. Musée national de Céramique, Sèvres: inv. CL. 7 482.

Among the attempts at coloured grounds some were not very successful. This curious piece has on the rim a design of polychrome flowers on a yellow-brown ground that has not spread very well. The subject in the centre is taken from the story of Elias as it is told in the Book of Kings. It shows Elias receiving loaves brought by crows. Below is written the exact reference to the Bible verses. This is evidently a rather coarse reproduction of an engraving.

134

135

136 Plate: delftware, high-temperature polychrome on a coloured ground, 3rd quarter of 18th century. D. 19 cm. Musées royaux d'Art et d'Histoire, Brussels: inv. 535, Evenepoël Collection.

The turquoise green glaze creates an exceptional ground allowing rare chromatic effects not unrelated to certain productions of northern France, but here, thanks to the transparent lead glaze (*kwaart*), there is a luminosity comparable to that of glass. All the effort seems to have been concentrated on handling this ground, against which four colours are to play: yellow, green, blue and black. In contrast, the motifs seem very hastily treated, both on the bottom, with a Chinaman sitting by the water, buildings and bushes, and on the rim, with almost illegible floral motifs. The shape is rather unusual for delftware with a very hollow centre and a notched edge to the rim.

136

137

137 Dish: delftware, high-temperature polychrome, *c.* 1730. D. 33.7 cm. Musée des Arts décoratifs, Paris: inv. D. 13 642.

The 'playing card' dishes were evidently highly popular, for several examples are known. The general effect is obtained by showing the fronts of some cards against the backs of others which have geometric patterns. This design spreads to the rim which is decorated with cupids in reserve on floral scrolls. The palette consists of red, blue, yellow and green. Two analogous dishes are preserved in the Musées royaux d'Art et d'Histoire, Brussels; they bear the dates 1731 and 1733 (*cf.* Helbig: *Faïences hollandaises,* p. 47); the rims alone differ.

Faïences with playing card decoration are famous, but generally, notably at Lille, they show a hand of royal or common sequence in a fan.

138 Lidded box or tobacco jar: delftware, blue-and-white, mark DEX (Jan Theunis Dextra, Greek A factory), *c.* 1770. H. 9.3 cm, D. 16.8 cm. Gemeente Museum, The Hague: inv. OCD. 100-1904, Van der Burgh Collection.

Cylindrical boxes with convex lids doubtless originate in porcelain: they were made in soft-paste at St Cloud, perhaps as early as the late seventeenth century; they must have served many purposes. This piece is called a tobacco jar because of the decoration: on the body are various scenes showing the preparation of tobacco; on the lid, framed in lambrequins, is a figure smoking a pipe. At the smoker's feet are spittoons in the Chinese style, the shape having also been used at Delft (Pl. 114). This blue-and-white is of fine quality, in spite of the late date of the piece.

138

139 Fountain and basin set: delftware, polychrome enamels, *c.* 1750. H. 39.5 cm. Rijksmuseum, Amsterdam: inv. 12 400 - 388.

For what seems to have been quite a short period, attempts were made at Delft to compete with European enamel-painted (*petit feu*) faïence and porcelain. These efforts resulted in the production of a variety of pieces, which have met with rather harsh criticism, particularly from F. Hudig. This fountain is a well-known and striking example of these wares. The painter and the potter are both trying to make a resolute break with the Oriental style and to follow the new rococo style in the shape of the basin and the contorted cartouches framing European landscapes. The influence of Japan breaks out, almost in spite of the painter, in the floral decoration and ornamental motifs.

'Motley' is the disparaging term sometimes directed at the extended range of colours used, probably because those versed in delftware are not accustomed to such variety in the palette.

140

140 Tureen with lid and dish: delftware, polychrome enamels, mark Z. Dex (Zacharias Dextra, Greek A factory), 3rd quarter of 18th century. H. 15 cm, D. of tray: 35 cm. Gemeente Museum, The Hague: inv. OCD. 31-1904, Van der Burgh Collection.

This well-known piece is one of the most striking examples of the efforts made by the potters at Delft to compete with European porcelain, abandoning the Oriental style. Following the principles of Meissen decoration, the genre scenes are set in gilt rococo cartouches, but it has to be noted that often this kind of faience has a greyish tinge to the glaze and rather dim gilding, as S.M. Voskuil-Groenewegen pointed out. The little subjects are treated in miniaturist style and the flowers are not lacking in quality.

141 Butter dish: delftware, polychrome enamels, mark V., *c.* 1735. H. 5 cm, W. 13 cm. Private collection, Paris.

A certain number of these boxes are known, in the form of an oval tub, always decorated in overglaze enamels and with European subjects. Pastoral scenes are the most frequent, as suits the function of the piece. The base is imagined as a basket. This type of decoration is usually thought to have resulted from the influence of the Meissen porcelain factory, but it should not be forgotten that pastoral scenes were in vogue at this time on all European pottery. The handle here is made of a voluted motif. Other such pieces have animals as handles. The mark, V., on the underside, is probably connected with the monogram V.A., which we see more often.

142 Coffee-pot: delftware, high-temperature polychrome, mid-18th century. H. 34.5 cm. Musée des Arts décoratifs, Paris: inv. D. 13 643.

The forms invented by the delftware potters include some unusual ideas during the eighteenth century, as though the purely exotic had ceased to attract sufficiently the taste of the shareholders (*winkelhouders*). This coffee-pot, with its pyramidal shape, the straight lines stressed by the bent rectilinear spout, looks quite peculiar when we reach the human feet on which it stands. It follows tradition in the usual Sino-Japanese motifs in the panels, already treated with less delicacy: a flowering hedge and a pagoda, made even less legible by being painted on the reeded surface.

143

143 Tureen with lid and tray: delftware, blue-and-white and polychrome, mark an axe (Porcelain Axe factory), late 18th century. Tray: L. 30 cm, W. 30 cm; tureen: H. 30 cm, L. 37 cm. Musée national de Céramique, Sèvres: 5 001.

This tureen with two handles illustrates both in form and in decoration the kind of efforts that were being made at Delft to find sources of inspiration other than those of the past. The shape, borrowed from metalwork, is rather different from its French equivalents, but the fruit-shaped knob recalls the knobs of pieces that were spread throughout Europe from Strasbourg. The naturalistic painting of this knob and the yellow stripe round the edge of the piece lend gaiety to the general effect. The decoration is of a type found all over northern Europe, with flowers and scrolls similar on both tureen and tray.

144 Coffee-pot: delftware, high-temperature polychrome, mid-18th century. H. 26.5. cm. Musée des Arts décoratifs, Paris: inv. D. 23 354.

The shape of this coffee-pot is quite as strange as that in Plate 143, but in a different way. The vessel swells towards the base and rests on three curved feet. A tap is fitted to the mouth of a human mask. The handles consist of two unidentifiable monsters with bird beaks. The tap seems rather incongruous, as we see the piece without the tripod on which it should stand so that a cup could be placed beneath it. The decoration emphasizes the shape of the profile. Broadly treated lambrequins surround the lower part and accentuate its generous form, while the upper part, with its slender branches, stresses the verticality of the form. A hook-shaped motif makes a very discreet appearance outlining what should be a 'perforated rock', in a manner tending towards rococo.

147

145

145 Pair of candlesticks: delftware, high-temperature polychrome, mark 'the Claw' (Porcelain Claw factory), 2nd half of 18th century. H. 27 cm. Musée national de Céramique, Sèvres: inv. CL. 7489 and CL. 7490.

These candlesticks can be cited as examples of the work of the period in which trompe-l'œil was combined with rococo style. Though they are decorated with high-temperature colours, every effort has been made to serve a kind of pseudo-naturalism such as is known in metalwork too at the same time. The polychrome effect is more important on the bases; the shaft in the form of a knotty trunk is done with effects of manganese, contrasting with the green of the foliage on the cups. The Claw mark used here would suggest the years 1760 to 1770.

146

◀ 146   Waisted vase: delftware, blue-and-white, mark H.L. (Jacobus Harlees), late 18th century. H. 40 cm. Musée national Adrien Dubouché, Limoges: inv. 988, Gasnault Collection.

The waisted vase with eight facets is highly typical of the garniture sets of the late period. As is indicated by the H.L. mark, the piece comes from the Porcelain Bottle factory at the time of Jacobus Harlees. We find all the decorative motifs of earlier times, but treated more conventionally; in the same way the Chinese unicorn (*qilin*) on the lid is hardly recognizable.

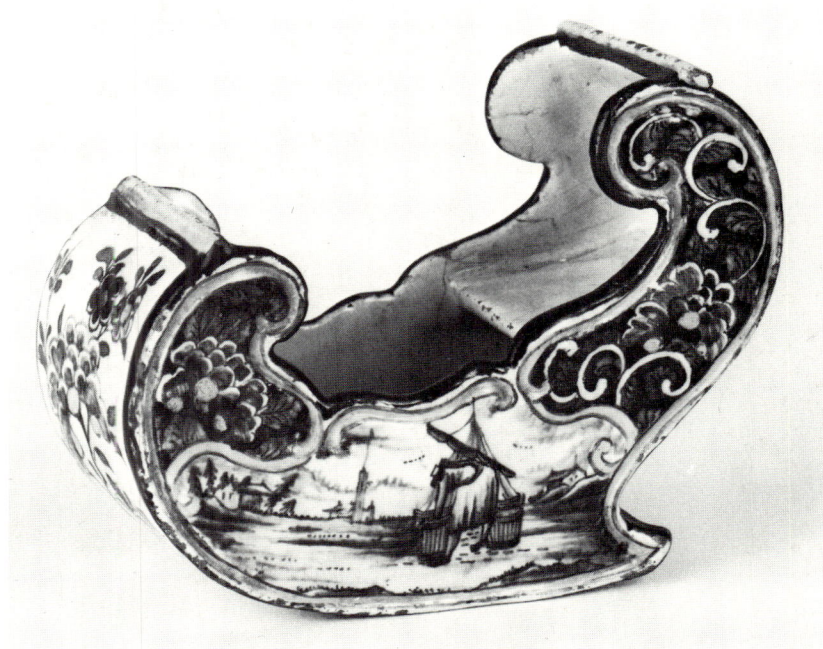

147

148

147   Sledge: delftware, high-temperature polychrome, *c.* 1740. L. 12.2. cm. Musée des Arts décoratifs, Paris: inv. D. 23 359.

During the eighteenth century, new forms began to appear in faience, some rather odd: shoes, brush handles, chests, sledges. On this one, the polychrome decoration in red, manganese, yellow and blue is treated in a hasty manner, but the picture of the little fisherman, painted in blue-and-white in an auricular scrolled panel, is not without its picturesque appeal. This form exists in blue-and-white, in both high-temperature and low-temperature painting, and in Delft *doré*. Sometimes a date is written on the seat.

148   Drug jar: delftware, blue-and-white, mark IP (Johannes Pennis), 18th century. H. 21.8 cm, W. 21.5 cm. Musée national de Céramique, Sèvres: inv. 21 451, Fombeure Bequest.

The Delft potteries supplied large numbers of apothecaries with jars. F. Hudig observes that these pharmacy jars must have appeared quite early at Delft, and the type of jar illustrated here, called a syrup jar (*strooppot*) figures in the regulations of the Guild of St Luke from 1654 as a subject of an examination, or master, piece for faience throwers. It appears, however, that none of the known jars goes back further than the late eighteenth century. Shapes and decoration hardly vary. Decoration consists mainly in the embellishment of the cartouche, either with two peacocks facing each other and flanking a vase of flowers, or more rarely a frieze of fish. The most usual marks are the Axe and L.P.K., for Lampet Kan.

VII 'PEASANT DELFT'

'Peasant Delft' is a ware that is rather distinctive in the way in which the decoration is treated. The general characteristic of these plates and dishes and a few closed-form pieces is a very broad style of painting with motifs so simplified that the Dutch have christened the ware 'peasant Delft' (*Boerendelftsch*). In many cases traditional themes are adopted, but the execution is less careful. The painting gives the impression that it is done in haste or by an apprentice. Perhaps these wares were intended to be fired in the least advantageous parts of the kiln. Because of the cost of a firing, no position was left empty, and the manufacturer placed pieces to be sold at lower prices in the parts of the kiln he knew were not the best. These wares were then sold more cheaply to a less demanding clientele. De Jonge observed that many pieces of 'peasant Delft' were used to decorate farm stables in the summer season when they were used for social gatherings.

It would be impossible to list all the different types of decoration done in this way in blue-and-white or five colours: rosette (a rather special kind), heart, lightning, hedge, bat, feather, fan, chimera, peacock and hind. We find it very surprising that our contemporaries have often failed to see how the spontaneity and naïvety of these large patches of colour with their crude drawing, based on a fine sense of design, can be of value to us.

This unsophisticated ware has much in common with topical designs. The usual example cited for this class is an early piece preserved in the Victoria and Albert Museum: a bowl decorated in the Oriental manner, referring in an inscription to the year of the Treaty of Ryswick, which ratified the end of the war between Holland, Spain, England and France.

It was quite a long time before political events reappeared on faience, but meanwhile there arose a satirical type of decoration that, paradoxically, reflects themes quite widespread in East India Company porcelain: holding up to ridicule the misfortunes of certain shareholders, and in not too refined a fashion. It is often said that these pieces refer to the victims of the law of bankruptcy, but that leaves unexplained why the inscriptions—not only on these faiences but on the Far Eastern wares—are always written in Dutch. We have already suggested that the satire was much more likely directed at the financial mishaps of the East India Company.

The best known type of the more popular wares is that coming under the heading of 'Orange' Delft. In the conflict at the end of the eighteenth century between the supporters of William V of Orange and those calling themselves 'patriots', the city of Delft seems to have taken sides with the chief of state (*stathouder*). Even earlier, there had been manifestations of support for the House of Orange. Apart from effigies of the princes, there are proclamations such as *Vivat Oranje - 1747*, signed with the monogram A.I.K.; and the number of dishes and plates (and rarer closed-form vessels) with decoration referring to the House of Orange shows how the Dutch potters held the family of Orange in affection. Many of the pieces, however, can be attributed to small Dutch factories and some even to English factories.

149

149 Dish: delftware, high-temperature polychrome, 18th century. D. 35.2 cm. Musée des arts décoratifs, Paris: inv. D. 17 087.

There is a whole body of wares based on the usual decorative principles but with its decoration very rapidly sketched, relying on colour for contrast: here green, blue and red. These pieces belong in the class of 'peasant Delft' (*Boerendelftsch*). They generally have abundant decoration intended to be seen at a distance. Dating this style of 'peasant Delft' is very difficult; it has been shown that it began in the late seventeenth century. Possibly the work was done by apprentices; many of these pieces must have been placed in the least suitable parts of the kiln.

150

150 Plate: delftware, high-temperature polychrome, 2nd half of 18th century. D. 30.2. cm. Musée national Adrien Dubouché, Limoges: inv. 1931 [4].

This 'peacock's tail' or 'fan' motif is very characteristic of the late production at Delft. It is known in very many examples, all with this strange structure that combines several indecipherable motifs. Round the edge, a motif reminiscent of Chinese 'clouds'. An attempt has sometimes been made to distinguish several categories according to the strength of the palette consisting of five colours, or according to the edge, which may be smooth or, as here, thickened and wavy.

151 Dish: delftware, high-temperature polychrome, 2nd half of 18th century. D. 35.2 cm. Musée des Arts décoratifs, Paris: inv. D. 17 087.

Pieces of this kind, relatively broad rimmed, are decorated with a series of very broadly treated motifs. The 'peacock' occurs frequently. It is painted here in yellow with blue ornaments, including its crest. The bird is surrounded by imaginary flowers and leaves. The 'large flower' recurs on the rim, painted in manganese and alternating in its panel with a narrower decorative motif. Some delicacy is achieved in the band of the cavetto with its bracket lobes. This piece is of 'peasant Delft' type.

151

152 Three plates: delftware, high-temperature polychrome, (bottom) both marked I.V.L. (Jan van der Laan?), lst half of 18th century, (top) dated 1749. D. 22 cm. Musée national de Céramique, Sèvres: Bottom: inv. 5 822a and 5 822b; Top: inv. 19 195, Petitet Donation.

What has been called 'peasant Delft' (*Boerendelftsch*) has rather different styles. Two plates have been put together here at the bottom which could be considered as prototypes of the genre. They are both signed I.V.L., which some have sought to attribute to Jan van der Laan, who worked in the Heart factory from the late seventeenth century. The quality varies greatly in this ware but the composition is always indisputably of great skill. These gaudy pieces demonstrate a many-sided decorative spirit. The plate on the bottom left can be thought of as already 'peasant' type, whereas the one on the bottom right still belongs to the fine tradition.

The plate at the top, with a woman beside a cradle, is related to the patriotic or 'Orangist' faiences. They are treated in a predominantly yellow palette, with blues and reds. The ingenuous and rustic inscription must refer to the birth of a prince. These pieces have sometimes been attributed to other factories than those at Delft, in Holland or even in England.

152

153

153 Plate: delftware, blue-and-white, 18th century. Musée des Arts décoratifs, Paris: inv. D. 23 218.

The group of pieces classified by the Dutch as 'peasant Delft' (*Boerendelftsch*), has decoration both in blue-and-white only and in polychrome. The most attractive type of the ware is certainly that with Oriental-style decoration. The themes are evidently the same as those used for more sophisticated work, but the spontaneity created by the speed of execution has a charm that in fact perhaps brings it closer to the aesthetic norms of the original model. This plate, with its stag and deer in a sketchily suggested landscape, framed by a scarcely more than adumbrated frieze, is based on the soundest decorative principles.

154 Plate: delftware, blue-and-white, c. 1720. D. 22 cm. Musée national Adrien Dubouché, Limoges: inv. 973, Gasnault Collection.

Delftware, like East India Company porcelain, produced a whole series of satirical figures with inscriptions satirizing unfortunate shareholders. Generally they are harlequins or mountebanks brandishing papers, always with a caption in Dutch. Some of these are ribald. Here 'Sotte Actien' refers to the madness of shareholders, spoken of by the Dutch as *Het Grote Tafereel der dwaasheid* (the great scene of madness). People have wondered whether the collapse of Law's System or the South Sea Bubble was meant by the reference. In fact, the two companies foundered at about the same time (1720). It may be that the Dutch were making fun of the victims of both events. The very simple border motifs correspond to the popular style of the piece.

VIII   FIGURINES, TROMPE-L'ŒIL AND FULL RELIEF

With such excellent raw material at his disposal, it is hardly surprising that the Delft potter started to experiment with moulds for modelling. The origins, all agree, go back to 1700 or earlier.

Several categories of objects, of widely different character, come under the heading of moulded figures. The imagination of the Dutch potter, which brought such fantasy to all his work, soon led to the appearance of trompe-l'œil. Boxes and tureens assumed amusing shapes. Many pieces represent farmyard poultry, buckets full of fish or vegetables. All these pieces betray the influence of France and Germany. *Pl. 156*

More peculiar to Holland are small oval boxes, many of which have lids in the form of a plover, while the box itself is portrayed as a more or less fantastic nest. They are called butter dishes, somewhat unconvincingly. Boxes with lids shaped as dab-fish are equally amusing. *Pl. 158*

Figures are often applied to objects as knobs or simply as ornaments on inkstands or candlesticks. *Pl. 155*

There are also the decorative figurines that corresponded to the general development of taste and clientele at Delft; it should be borne in mind, however, that no one type was ever completely abandoned. The first models were Far Eastern: half Chinese half Japanese. We find little Chinese deities, among them a few, very rare Guanyins or little aggressive-looking grotesques. Chinese influence is even more direct on animal sculpture. The parrot perched on a dome-shaped 'perforated rock', one of the most common biscuit pieces of the Kangxi period, is reproduced almost exactly. Only the palette varies slightly, the Delft painter substituting other colours for the famous Chinese aubergine-purple. Cocks are also a direct copy of Asiatic models. These may be entirely polychrome or partly black, partly polychrome. Horses have a very Chinese look and may be glazed in either black or polychrome. The black ground also gave rise to curious depictions of Negro servants. *Pl. 160* *Pl. 159* *Pls. 97, 162*

However, a different style gradually appeared during the eighteenth century, certainly under the influence of various foreign faience and porcelain factories. Its naïvety gives it a certain charm. There are many figures, but the best known models are probably the oxen and cows decorated in various techniques: high-temperature polychrome, Delft *doré*, enamelling. It has been said that, originally, this representation of a bovid with hoofs and horns (sometimes gilded) was connected with a special festival at Delft, a city in which the butchers played an important role, and that some of the best specimens of cattle-rearing were led in procession round the streets. However, inspiration from dairy farming seems to be rather more likely in view of the existence of groups with a man or a woman in the process of milking. *Pl. 161*

There are the other naturalistic animal figures simulating the porcelains and faiences of Strasbourg, Niderviller, Meissen, Chantilly, etc., and they include boar, stags, deer. *Pl. 157*

There is an endless variety of little people: musicians, mountebanks, street sellers or pedlars. There are also young ladies and gentlemen in Louis XV costume, decorated mostly in enamels. *Pls. 162-3*

Towards the end of the production, under the influence of French biscuit ware, figures were made in white glaze, and De Jonge mentions a reproduction by the Vincennes factory of the *Little Girl with a Cage*, after Boucher, which she dates to about 1760 (Gemeente Museum, Arnhem).

Some of the strangest objects, which have interested even non-specialists in faience, are the amazing violins that faithfully reproduce the real instrument. Four are famous: in the Rijksmuseum; the Gemeente Museum, The Hague; the Musée du Conservatoire national de Musique, Paris and the Musée des Beaux-Arts, Rouen. They contain very finely executed decoration, with concert scenes, musical emblems and designs that connect *Pl. 165*

Pl. 164 these pieces with the most glorious age of European decoration, still influenced by Daniel Marot.

Pl. 166 Henry Havard made a cautious suggestion that there was a connection between these exceptional pieces and the armorial furniture of the family he calls Van der Hoeve (and the Dutch Van der Houve). Several members of that family were said to be master faience potters, and the author adds, 'the Van der Hoeve bore in their coat of arms three violins sable on a field argent....' Several pieces with these arms are known (see Pl. 166).

Some busts were made in the seventeenth century, as proved by a pair of portrait busts signed 'Jan Decker 1698', preserved in the Musées royaux d'Art et d'Histoire, Brussels. There are also effigies of members of the House of Orange. Pl. 167

Pure sculpture sometimes gave rise to rather dubious attempts at reproduction, such as of the Vatican *Il Spinario* or Raphael's *Wax Figure*, both of which were reduced to miniatures about 20 centimetres high. Pl. 168

155

155 Lidded box: delftware, high-temperature polychrome, c. 1740. D. 15 cm, H. 13 cm. Private collection.

This type of circular box was the occasion of very varied decoration. Its purpose is not always certain: usually called either a comfit or tobacco box. Though it is very simple, the floral decoration is elegant, as is the shape. It is done with great delicacy in four colours: yellow, red, manganese-purple and blue. The knob on the lid is in the form of a little kneeling Chinaman and lends a special note to the whole aspect of the piece.

156

156 Lidded tureen with its dish: delftware, high-temperature polychrome, mark I: S, 3rd quarter of 18th century. H. 32 cm, D. of dish 45 cm. Musées royaux d'Art et d'Histoire, Brussels: inv. 724, Evenepoël Collection.

This is a very peculiar shape of tureen, composed of a vessel with a flaring profile and very simple foliage decoration, surmounted by a coiled pike. The lid is a second pike swallowing a small fish. The dish too, which is quite deep, has a rim in the form of two more pike. This is an unusually strange construction, though a number of vessels are known with trompe-l'œil pike, ranging from butter dishes to large tureens. The palette here is quite restricted (green, yellow and manganese-purple). The initials I : S on this piece are not of any known factory, but similar pieces have some of the most frequent marks of the second half of the eighteenth century.

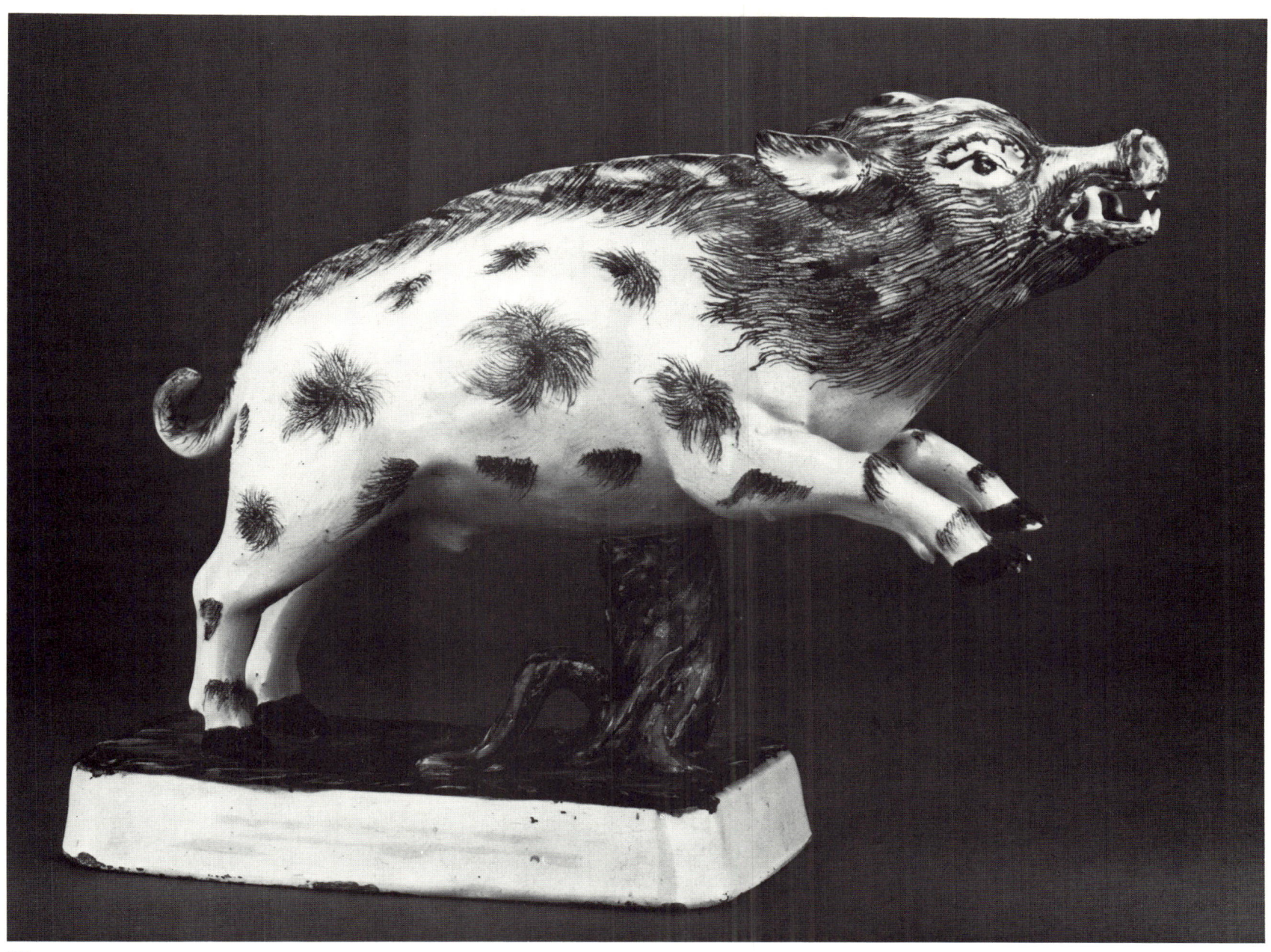

157

157 Leaping boar: delftware, high-temperature polychrome, 2nd half of 18th century. L. 26 cm. Gemeente Museum, The Hague: inv. OCD. 106 - 1904.

The figure is in a special ware, belonging to a series of animal figures which, though they sought to compete with certain European enamel wares, only made use of a very limited number of colours: here manganese-purple and a little red. This type of boar is reminiscent of the Strasbourg figures, or of Höchst or Meissen figurines, which are mostly items for table centres, combining huntsmen, horses, dogs and game to make a hunting scene.

158

158 Two plover boxes: delftware, high-temperature polychrome, mark I.T.D./12 (Jan Theunis Dextra), *c.* 1765. L. 15 cm, W. 11 cm. Private collection.

The plethora of different forms characteristic of the second half of the eighteenth century quite often stimulated inventions connected with the idea of trompe-l'œil, perhaps under foreign influence. Sometimes these objects reflect local customs more closely, for instance there are a number of these boxes with lids in the form of plovers and pots depicting nests. The painting in blue, green and manganese-purple aims at naturalism. The mark I.T.D. over a 12 is well known: it belongs to Jan Theunis Dextra, who worked at the Greek A factory and is considered to be one of the best delftware potters of the second part of the eighteenth century. C.H. de Jonge dates this mark precisely to 1764. Pieces of this kind bear other marks, such as that of Van Duyn.

159 Cock: delftware, high-temperature polychrome, early 18th century. H. 19.6 cm. Gemeente Museum, The Hague: inv. OCD. 204-1904, Van der Burgh Collection.

Figures of cocks are quite numerous, doubtless made by different factories in imitation of Chinese porcelains. They give scope for a subtle play of colours. It should be possible to distinguish several types, perhaps even a development, particularly from the manner of treating the terrace forming the base: it is either an irregular mound or, as here, a real stand enhanced with a special decoration. The size is not always the same, but the bird is always similar. Generally, this type of figure has no mark, but there are a few exceptions with the monogram of Pieter Adriaensz Kocks or of Lambertus van Eenhoorn.

159

160

160 Parrot: delftware, high-temperature polychrome, *c.* 1730. H. 24 cm. Musées royaux d'Art et d'Histoire, Brussels: inv. 11, Evenepoël Collection.

The Chinese potters of the Kangxi period (1662-1722) produced quite a number of these parrots perched on a 'perforated rock' in the so-called 'biscuit technique'. They used it as an opportunity to exploit the play of different colours. These birds found a ready appreciation among the delftware potters, who began to copy them, also setting them on a bell-shaped base. This is one of the most faithful imitations of Far Eastern porcelain.

161 Pair of cows: delftware, Delft *doré,* 2nd quarter of 18th century. H. ▶ 15 cm. Rijksmuseum, Amsterdam: inv. 12 400 - 338/339, Loudon Collection.

The butchers' guild is known to have been very influential at Delft; its guildhouse, still in existence, is illustrated on a plaque (Pl. 34). We have been told how on feast days the finest beasts were decorated with flowers for the procession; they even had gilded horns and hoofs. The many depictions of cows must be connected with this kind of celebration. They have been rendered in every technique of decoration: high-temperature colours, Delft *doré* and enamels, but because of their celebrity they were much reproduced in the nineteenth century in the factories. It is important, therefore, to examine the quality of the modelling and the authenticity of the glazes.

161

163

162 Figurine: delftware, high-temperature polychrome, mark J.G. (Jan Gaal), 1st quarter of 18th century. H. 18 cm. Musée national Adrien Dubouché, Limoges: inv. 2 431.

Though they look rather naïve, a number of high-temperature painted figurines show the European inspiration still marked by Far Eastern traditions, particularly in the treatment of the horse (*cf.* Pl. 97). The rider, obviously an addition, shows clearly that the sculptor had little practice in modelling human figures, the arms being treated more like handles. The base has the usual polychrome painting. The mark J.G. is given by C.H. de Jonge as that of Jan Gaal, who worked until about 1725 in the Two Little Ships factory.

162

163 Figurine: delftware, high-temperature polychrome, mark J.G. /8 (Jan Gaal), 1st quarter of 18th century. H. 38 cm. British Museum, London: inv. 1820.3.18.17.

This type of figurine is rather exceptional; it probably formed part of an ensemble for table decoration. Though from the same workshop, the modelling is superior to that of the horseman of Plate 162. On a little platform decorated with blue and red fleurons stands a figure in fancy dress, such as was often portrayed at the time, intended to symbolize a trade. If the figure is turned round it can be seen that the trousers and sleeves represent jugs, and the torso the top of a barrel from which leaves and fruit emerge. On his head he is wearing a hat in the shape of a plant, and he is holding a bottle in one hand and a bowl in the other, all evoking wine. This is a ballet costume of the kind much in vogue.

163

165

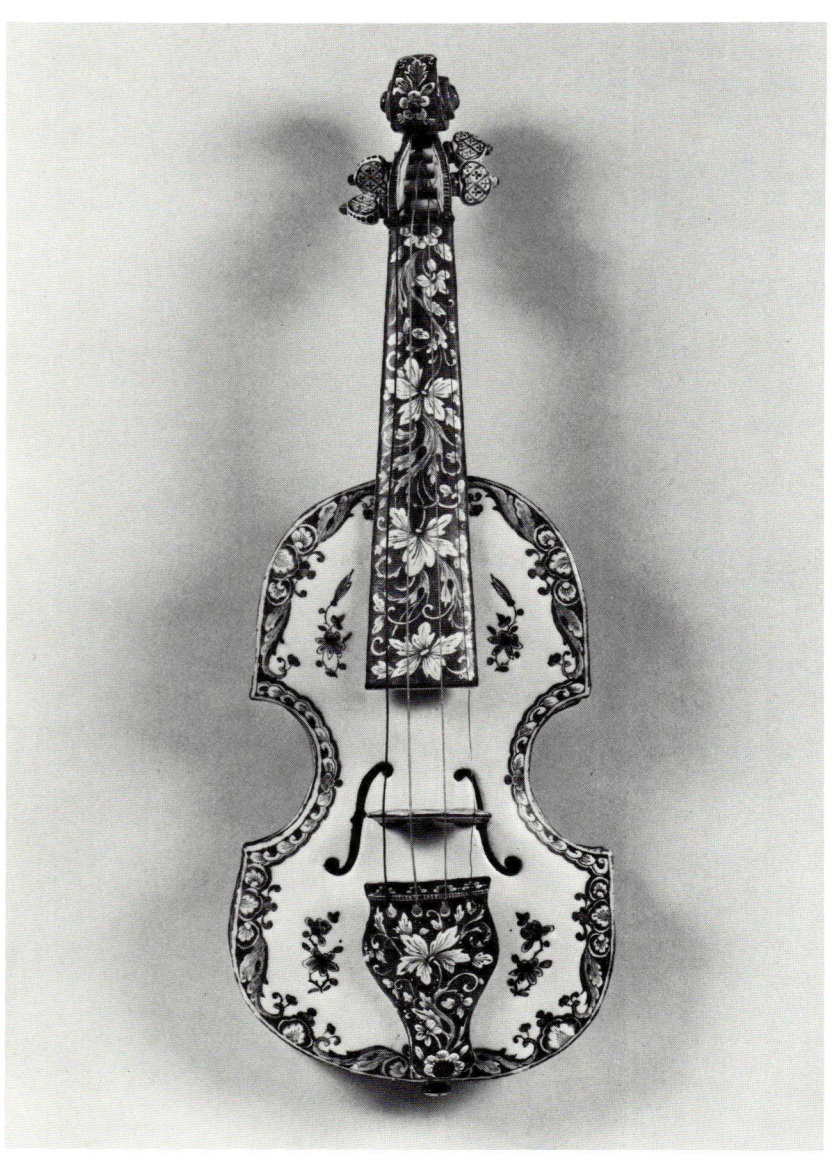

164   Violin: delftware, blue-and-white, *c.* 1725. L. 61. 7 cm. Musée du Conservatoire national de Musique, Paris: inv. E206-C23.

This violin, less well known but quite as beautifully made as the violin in the Musée des Beaux-Arts, Rouen (Pl. 165) has a very different decoration, in Oriental style: 'perforated rocks', flowering sprays and parrots adorn the back while neck and scroll have lambrequins and floral scrolls in reserve. Henry Havard suggested amusingly that these violins were connected with the Van der Hoeve family (*cf.* Pl. 166) whose crest bore three violins. Some confusion in the interpretation of the archives is possible, for a Van der Houve family also made delftware, but the fact certainly remains that the presence of the arms with three violins on certain pieces has to be reckoned with.

165   Violin: delftware, blue-and-white, *c.* 1725. L. 62 cm. Musée des Beaux-Arts, Rouen.

Faience violins are a well-known genre on which the potter's virtuosity was lavished. Four are preserved in public institutions: one in the Rijksmuseum, another in the Musées royaux d'Art et d'Histoire, Brussels, a third in the Musée du Conservatoire national de Musique, Paris (*cf.* Pl. 164), and the fourth, shown here, in the Musée des Beaux-Arts, Rouen. It was probably this one that inspired a charming story, *Le violon de faïence*, by the novelist Champfleury who was Curator in the Musée national de Céramique, Sèvres, in the nineteenth century. The requirements of violin making are scrupulously observed, and the back and belly are used by the faience painter to display a design of the highest quality. The decoration of the belly, here, is evidently inspired from an architectural design in which the sound holes are included so that their curves emphasize the outlines of the baroque construction. The whole composition, with two winged genii standing out at its base holding a shield with the dove of the Holy Ghost, and two putti under an arch at the top, frames a musical trophy. The design on the back is equally interesting, with players round a spinet. The women wear the 'fontange' head-dress made fashionable by the mistress of Louis XIV, Marie de Fontange. Eight little cherub musicians are shown in a cloud, and above them floats an angel bearing a banderole with the inscription: *Musica Gloriam Aer(is)*. The paintings are done with a delicacy reminiscent (though later) of Van Frÿtom. The dark outlines (*trek*) are hardly visible.

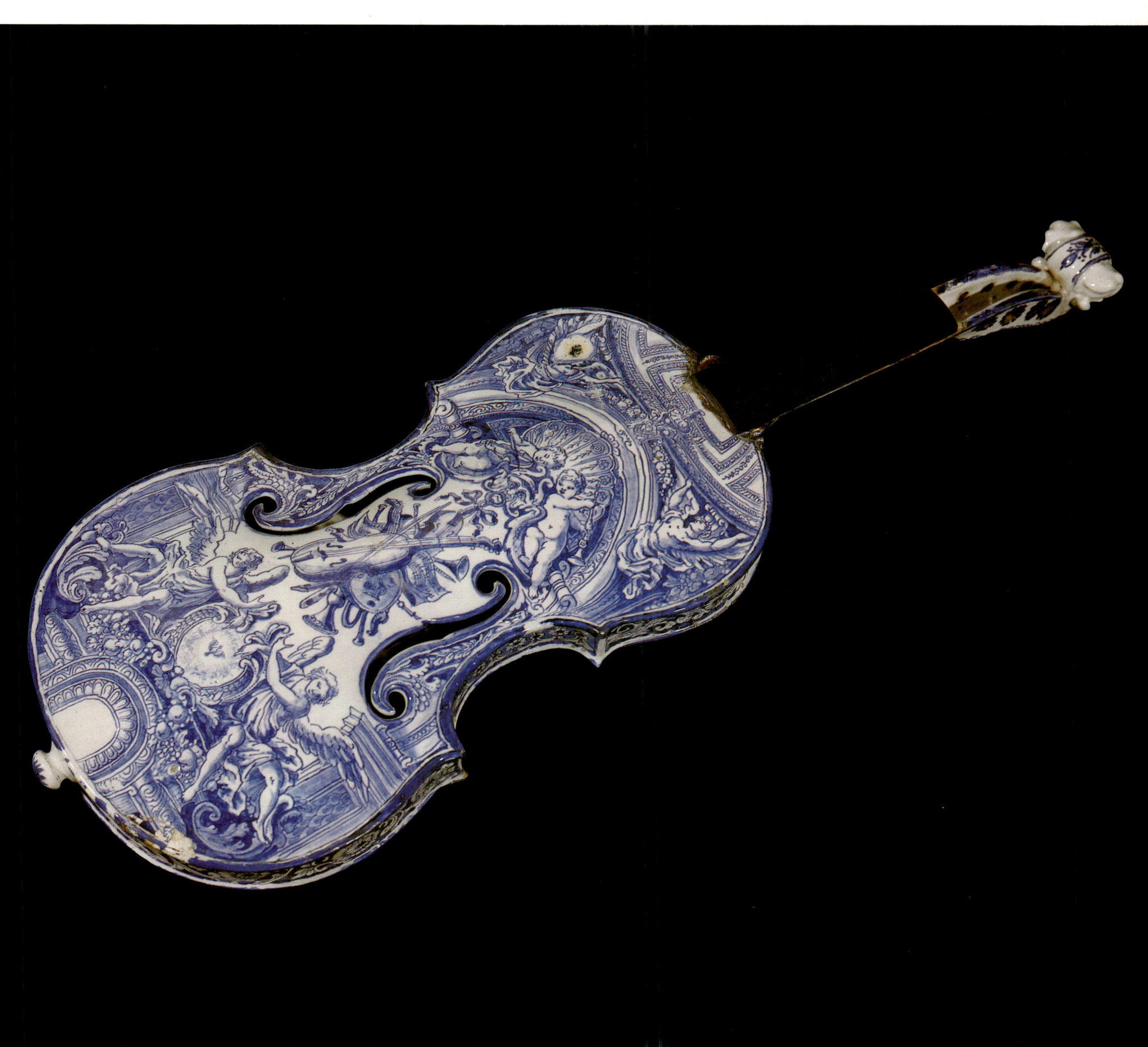

166

166 Wall plaque: delftware, blue-and-white, c. 1720. H. 37.5 cm, W. 21.5 cm. Musée national Adrien Dubouché, Limoges: inv. 996, Gasnault Collection.

167 Crowned bust: delftware, blue-and-white, mark Jan Decker, dated 1698. H. 28.5 cm. Musées royaux d'Art et d'Histoire, Brussels: inv. 730b, Evenepoël Collection.

The plaque illustrated here has a remarkable variety of motifs. The main design in the usual Japanese style similar to Imari ware contrasts with the richness of the framing decoration, with its volutes, tassels and heads against a chequered ground, and above it the crown of a marquis over the shield flanked by lions. The arms with three violins were already mentioned by Henry Havard as those of the Van der Hoeve family: 'bearing three violins sable on a ground argent....' Several pieces are known with this rather unusual device. The banderole below the escutcheon can be read more or less: *Willem. van. der. Hy eve*. Havard's hypothesis that this relates to the Van der Hoeve or rather Van der Houve, who were potters at Delft, may seem rather hazardous.

One of a pair, this bust is very odd. It seems to be the work of a potter more skilled in decoration than in sculpting. The signature, *Jan Decker-1698,* drew the attention of Henry Havard who wrote: 'I have been able to find out very little about Decker. The Dutch registry office only provides the information that he married late, a Claartie Sibecker (alias Clara Siepperker) who bore him half a dozen children (1729 to 1744)....' Very little indeed! The cupid among flowers on the plinth, the abundance of ornament on the garment are of a quality well in accordance with the last years of the seventeenth century.

168 Figurine: delftware, high-temperature polychrome, mark G.N. and I.R., *c.* 1720. H. 16 cm. Musées royaux d'Art et d'Histoire, Brussels: inv. 123, Evenepoël Collection.

This little figurine is rather unusual, with its imitation of classical sculpture, in this case the famous Vatican figure *Il Spinario*. The softness of the modelling gives it an unusual look, to which an amusing note is added by the supporting base: the drapery of the plinth, the monster's head on which the boy's foot is resting are painted in a rich palette of yellow, blue and red, all bearing witness to the irrepressible fantasy of the Delft potter. The initials G.N. and I.R. in blue have not been explained. The suggestion of Guillaume Nieullet put forward by Havard cannot be accepted.

IX ORNAMENTAL PLAQUES

Plaques were made in many centres other than Delft, of course, but the imaginative Delft painters applied their skills to the ornamental plaque, creating paintings of particularly notable delicacy.

Several different approaches were made in this genre. We saw elsewhere (pp. 21, 24) how Frederik van Frÿtom and Gÿsbrecht Verhaast treated rectangular plaques in the manner of painters or engravers. Nearer the ceramic style are the splendid decorative panels with compositions taken from Daniel Marot but still consisting of an assemblage of tiles. More in the spirit of Van Frÿtom, on the other hand, are some little pictures in blue-and-white, usually representing monuments or street scenes.

Decorative plaques independent of the idea of tiling stand in a class apart. The origins are usually dated to about 1675. The plaque is oval, and the edge is raised to form a frame. These are the plaques on which the flower pieces (*bloemendekor*) appeared that are considered the first manifestation of polychromy at Delft. [Pl. 49]

The shape of the plaque altered as the style developed, but the plain edged oval was prevalent in the early eighteenth century. Some of the purest masterpieces of delftware belong to this category. Along with blue-and-white plaques, sometimes with a mixture of European and Far Eastern motifs, we find polychrome pieces, notably [Pl. 64] 'slender ladies', and some black grounds. [Pls. 88-9]

It is very difficult to date the elaborations in the outline of the oval plaque, for some of the best pieces with 'slender ladies' have lobed frames and still belong to the early eighteenth century. The compositions are organized either vertically (in which case they must often have been made in pairs) or horizontally. Perhaps it is later in the eighteenth century that we begin to find the more elaborate frame with volutes and scrolls, resting on shells [Pl. 171] in relief. The subject is still very classical in character: vases and baskets of flowers rest on the heads of cupids or monsters, all supported on a complicated structure with spokes and volutes.

In time, these plaques—to which the Delft potters remained faithful—abandoned the principle of symmetry, and combinations in rococo taste began to be used to frame genre scenes of a very un-Dutch character.

The plaque, mentioned in the discussion of shapes, was used as a support for a candlestick. A ring is placed [Pls. 166, 173] at the bottom to hold the curved branch of the chandelier. Not many faience branches have survived; possibly some of them were made of metal.

The somewhat ingenuous idea of using a plaque simulating a bird cage belongs to the less sophisticated, late [Pl. 170] period of Delft production. It had some vogue, being fitted into a tiled wall. The tiles surrounding it would be cut back to make the plaque appear as a trompe-l'œil.

In this second half of the eighteenth century, the ornamental plaque was used for the most varied and unexpected purposes. Clock faces or mobile panels with hands (used as calendars) are examples. More pleasing are some plaques painted with charming heads of girls, sketched [Pl. 172] like a pencil drawing and often in very refined taste.

169

169 Plaque: delftware, high-temperature polychrome, *c.* 1720. H. 22.5 cm. Musée des Arts décoratifs, Paris: inv. D.23 383.

The colours on this plaque are as rich and full as those of Plate 79. The motif of a Chinaman hunting with his bow is similar in spirit to the one on the Hoppesteyn sweetmeat (pickle) dish (*cf.* Pl. 43). The motifs added to fill the irregular areas created by the indented frame are curiously conceived, with variegated hangings on one side and foliage growing from rocks on the other; at the base of the design are plant motifs including the kind of heather twig that came from China; they are also found on Frankfurt faience, or Nevers, but painted here in bright red. Above is a branch-like decoration in the same red.

170 Shaped plaque: delftware, high-temperature polychrome, c. 1750-60. H. 45 cm. Musée des Arts décoratifs, Paris: inv. D. 17 094.

171 Plaque with indented outline: delftware, high-temperature polychrome, 2nd quarter of 18th century. H. 36 cm, W. 33 cm. Private collection.

The bird-cage shaped plaque was for setting in a wall, probably among tiles. The production of such shapes was very special work. An effect of trompe-l'œil was obviously intended. The style of this piece is strange: on the one hand we have the effects of drapery and tasselled cords, the trimmings attached in the early eighteenth-century manner; on the other, at the base of the cage, is the framed, French style scene of gallantry, flanked in the traditional manner by two Chinamen, typically rococo, a much later style.

This taste for bird-cages was exploited often, not only at Delft but in other northern factories, notably at Lille. Of all the cages made at Delft, this is one of the most elaborate. Quite often the upper part was a simple dome, making the production and mounting much easier.

Vases of flowers are a frequent motif on ornamental plaques, but sometimes the composition is out of the ordinary. This is a bizarre construction composed of monstrous heads and consoles with a chequered pattern of various colours. The frame itself, alternately blue, red and yellow, is a foil for the painter's irresistible fantasy. It is exceptional to see such elaborate treatment in the handling of the blues and polychrome. The design is probably based on the vignettes proper to graphic art. The same motif is found, somewhat simplified, on a dish preserved in the Musées royaux d'Art et d'Histoire, Brussels (Evenepoël Coll.: 508).

171

172

172 Rectangular plaque: delftware, blue-and-white, 2nd half of 18th century. H. 34 cm, W. 26 cm. Private collection.

This decorative plaque, forming a picture in blue-and-white in a manganese-brown frame, is a good example of the influence of French styles on delftware in the mid-eighteenth century. This charming Boucher-style figure belongs to a whole mannered trend, which at times reveals a somewhat libertine spirit. The theme here, with its piquant little incident, is a standard one. The painter's skill in respecting the drawing of the artist is considerable. Some ribbons show traces of the pricking.

173 Plaque with indented outline: delftware, polychrome enamels, ▶
c. 1755. H. 37.7 cm. Musée des Arts decoratifs, Paris: inv. D. 30 425.

These plaques, some of which have a ring for holding a light, are in the rococo auricular style, with asymmetrical outline, volutes and shells (cf. Pl. 166). The decoration here is treated in bright colours, not unlike gouache. The pastoral scene is certainly taken from the pastoral paintings (bergeries) of Nicolas Berghem, which had an enormous influence on the decorators of the period. The famous faience painter Nicolas Anstett was inspired by him, first at Strasbourg then at Niderwiller. A rather curious decorative effect, probably the painter's own invention, is the way the willow branches fall from the top as though from the shell.

174

X DUTCH TILES

It is still often thought that most Dutch tiles were made at Delft. In fact, it has long been known that the majority of the splendid tiles decorating palace and house walls come from other Dutch towns. The idea of using ceramic tiles for ornament in this way obviously reached the Netherlands through Spain, which had inherited it from the Near East. Proof of this lies in the fact that the manufacture of Dutch tiles goes back much earlier than the origins of faience-making at Delft. There is, therefore, no question of making a profound study of Dutch tiles in this book, but we must at least mention the fact that part of Dutch majolica consisted of this kind of production.

As in all the history of Dutch faience, the workshops of Antwerp represent the beginnings; the pavements of *The Vyne* in Hampshire (England) and of the Abbey of Herckenrode in Limbourg (Belgium) are the most famous examples. In these tiles, the inspiration is more Italian than Spanish; they are the work of Guido di Savino's kiln. It is in the early seventeenth century that one can see a stronger Spanish influence, all the more apparent when paving tiles were replaced by wall tiles.

Designs composed of stylized leaves in reserve (on alternately blue and green or orange grounds) generally form combinations in fours.

Other types of designs appeared quite early: animals or sometimes human figures on sketched-out terraces, all set in circular medallions in reserve on a blue ground, embellished with fleurons also in reserve. This style of decoration changed about 1620, when it is thought there first appeared a strange new composition: a central medallion inscribed within an irregular convoluted frame like Chinese panels; the fleurons are replaced by geometric motifs in blue on white, also reminiscent of the Far East.

Parallel with these types of decoration are other compositions, framed or all-over: vases filled with tulips and carnations or bowls filled with grapes and pomegranates.

The production of tiles continued throughout the seventeenth and eighteenth centuries. The iconography was inexhaustible: birds, little figures and, above all, seascapes, sometimes treated in polychrome but usually in blue-and-white. Attributions of tiles are always difficult: Rotterdam, Haarlem, Gouda, Utrecht and Amsterdam produced them in great numbers, not to mention the Frisian factories.

The idea of composing a picture from a number of separate tiles must have started early (a panel of 1594 is known). They became more common towards the second quarter of the seventeenth century. One very well-known type can be identified because of a signature dating to around 1700. This is the seascape done in bold broad brushwork by Cornelis Boumeester, who worked at Rotterdam and was active between 1693 and 1733. He generally used the inscription C.B.M. on a floating barrel. This potter also painted mythological scenes. *Pl. 174*

We must pause for a moment too at another well-known genre of panel which is often attributed to Delft. These are sumptuous compositions in blue-and-white or polychrome with a large 'Medici'-type vase holding an opulent pyramid of flowers and surrounded by birds and butterflies. These splendid panels have given rise to much comment. If they really come from Delft itself, they must be the work of the Rose factory. De Jonge dates them to the years around 1720. Examples of such panels still remain *in situ*, in France at the château of Rambouillet and in Bavaria in the kitchen of the hunting lodge of Amalienburg near Nymphenburg. The Bavarian panels have different subjects: either the floral compositions described above or more Oriental decoration, with Chinese figures fighting or riding among pagodas, and other totally fantastical 'Oriental' scenes, all in very strong colours (even including black). These panels are framed by series of tiles made in the Flowerpot (*Bloempot*) factory of Rotterdam. *Pl. 176*

174

174 Panel of 54 tiles: Rotterdam faience, blue-and-white, mark C:B M (Cornelis Pieterszn Boumeester), early 18th century. H. 78 cm, W. 91 cm. Musée national de Céramique, Sèvres: inv. 20 739, Landeau Donation.

Rotterdam was certainly one of the centres that produced the greatest quantity of tiles. Cornelis Pieterszn Boumeester is probably the best known manufacturer. One of the reasons for this is that he often signed his works with his cipher; most of them were seascapes. This one is drawn directly from contemporary paintings. Boumeester's initials often appear, as here, on a floating barrel. There are rarer panels signed by him in full, with pictures of mythological subjects (Musées royaux d'Art et d'Histoire, Brussels).

175 Panel of 58 tiles: delftware (?), high-temperature polychrome, early 18th century. H. 170 cm. Rijksmuseum, Amsterdam: inv. 12 400-443, Loudon Collection.

This, with the panel in the Musées royaux d'Art et d'Histoire, Brussels, and those in the hunting pavilion of Amalienburg at Nymphenburg in Bavaria, is one of the most remarkable tile panels in composition and intensity of colour range. The palette is very close to that used in the Rose factory. F. Hudig in *Delfter Fayence,* p. 158, writes about this panel: 'The Dutch were great travellers and developed a cosmopolitan decoration with dancing niggers mingled with Chinese, while over them Guanyin seated on a red lotus throne surrounded by yellow rays pours a firework of colours from her flask containing gifts full of blessings....' In fact, the figures painted in black are, according to C. H. de Jonge, Tapuya Indians, made fashionable in the seventeenth century by the pictures of Albert van Eekhout. The painter seems to have used the presence of these figures among the Chinese to give greater value to black in the middle of his palette, with the naïve notion of being exotic.

175

176 Panel of 108 tiles: delftware (?), high-temperature polychrome decoration, *c.* 1720. H. 172 cm, W. 91 cm. Musée national de Céramique, Sèvres: inv. 7 221.

This and similar panels have been much written about. This one is compared to four panels which are very much like it; they were installed between 1715 and 1730 in the Château de Rambouillet, commissioned by the Count of Toulouse. This panel should also be compared to the floral panel in blue-and-white now preserved in the Rijksmuseum, which came from the bed-chamber of the director of an orphanage at Sommelsdijk in Holland, where it is said to have been set up in 1722 above a fireplace. There are also polychrome panels to which this one has been compared: two in the Rijksmuseum, one in the Victoria and Albert Museum and three *in situ* in the kitchen of the hunting lodge of Amalienburg at Nymphenburg near Munich; the latter had a complicated history and were not installed until 1739 (*cf.* C. H. de Jonge, *Delft Ceramics,* pp. 169-71). In fact, all these panels seem to date from about 1720. They are so similar that they are probably the work of the same factory; the most convincing attribution is to the Rose factory. All the panels correspond quite closely to the so-called 'flower piece'(*bloemen dekor*) type: a dense piling up of flowers and birds forming a bouquet rising from a Medici vase standing on a pedestal. Here, on each side, are two smaller vases of flowers; on other pieces there are birds. In every case the elegance of the composition and the extraordinary crowding of the flowers, reminiscent of the *mille fleurs* decoration of Chinese porcelain, combined with the classical shape of the vase, show that a mature stage of production has been reached.

XI DUTCH FAIENCE OTHER THAN DELFTWARE

So little is known of the other Dutch factories, all of which, during the eighteenth century, tended to imitate the great centre at Delft, that there is a danger of mistaken attributions unless we mention them in connection with our studies of delftware. Sufficient attention is rarely paid to them. Other than Delft, the main places where faience was made are Arnhem, Haarlem, Middelburg, Rotterdam and in Frisia at Harlingen, Leeuwarden, Makkum and Bolsward.

The great specialist in Frisian ware was Nanne Ottema. He drew attention to the early date (sixteenth century) of some centres such as Harlingen and Leeuwarden. Bolsward is known specially for a blue-and-white plaque preserved in the Rijksmuseum, with a picture of a faience factory, dated 1737. But Makkum seems to be the most interesting centre, and its main factory survived into the twentieth century. It was founded by Freerk Jans Tichelaar, in 1675, and managed to stand up to the competition from Delft. Neurdenburg describes Makkum ware as having a chalky glaze and a duller blue than delftware. Some decorations very similar to delftware of the second half of the eighteenth century are often attributed to Makkum, showing biblical or mythological subjects and above all seascapes. The rims of dishes have very simplified motifs. The tradition of faience at Haarlem goes back to Adriaen Bogaert in the sixteenth century.

Arnhem faience, with its cock mark, is more easily recognizable. It was studied in depth by J.M. Noothoven van Goor. The Arnhem factory was founded by Johan van Kerckhoff, in 1759. The style is really rather different from delftware with a strong influence of 'French' taste. The signboard plaque in the Musées royaux d'Art et d'Histoire, Brussels, is well known, with a genre scene in blue-and-white after an engraving by Nilson. It shows a picture of the factory. The whole decoration is set under a banderole inscribed 'Arnhemse Fabrique', and above it is a cock, recalling the factory mark. The few pieces of Arnhem ware known so far show by the finish in both form and decoration that they were designed for a clientele of some refinement.

---

177 Dish: Frisian faience, blue-and-white, dated 1780. D. 35 cm. Musée national Adrien Dubouché, Limoges: inv. 2 399.

The various Frisian factories produced abundantly in the second half of the eighteenth century, causing much confusion among earlier scholars. Though some features of Dutch style are evident, the wares differ in many points from delftware. Many of the faience factories specialized to some extent in tiles, and the Frisian painters tended to treat the decoration of dishes in the same manner. In this seascape, the treatment of the clouds is notable. On this topic F. Hudig writes in *Delfter Fayence*: 'The treatment of cloud strata is also characteristic of this Frisian style of decoration....' The rim is probably the work of a different painter and bears flower scrolls of quite good quality.

178 Dish: delftware (?), high-temperature polychrome, early 18th century. D. 39 cm. Musée national de Céramique, Sèvres: inv. 6 248, Meusnier Donation.

This portrait of King Frederick of Prussia riding on the battlefield is not treated in a typical Delft manner. The very restricted palette consists of orange-brown and green, which are only used in touches to set off the blue. The blue is not the regular expanse of special Delft colour. The face with its over-large eyes emphasized with a heavy dab of blue is similar to the treatment on other pieces, among them a jug preserved in the Musées royaux d'Art et d'Histoire, Brussels, dated 1675. Some experts think these pieces come from a Dutch centre other than Delft.

177

178

179

179 Coffee-pot: Arnhem faience, blue-and-white, Cock mark, c. 1760. H. 36.5 cm. Musées royaux d'Art et d'Histoire, Brussels: inv. 16, Evenepoël Collection.

The factory founded at Arnhem by Johan van Kerckhoff (1759-73) has been very carefully studied by J.M. Noothoven van Goor. In its short period of activity it produced extremely fine faience, most bearing the mark of a cock. This form of three-legged coffee-pot with a tap was common. Like the delftware pieces, it was intended to stand on a tripod. The pastoral scene is strongly influenced by French engravings. The blue in which it is painted is very delicate and graded.

XII THE ROLE AND INFLUENCE OF DELFTWARE IN EUROPE

The four main centuries in the history of European faience saw a succession of phases, each characterized by the dominating influence on faience at the time. As the heir to a technique discovered within the framework of Islamic civilization, the first European faience reflected its origins: Hispano-Moresque faience of the fourteenth and fifteenth centuries. Majolica, in turn, spread its influence, and the word faience is a telling indication of the extent to which Faenza, Italy, disseminated its products and style throughout Renaissance Europe. The third phase dates from the second half of the seventeenth century. Its inspiration is Far Eastern, and now delftware begins to play a major role. Its influence could be traced into almost every European country. We shall restrict ourselves to reviewing its effects in three only: the German states, England and France.

The German states must have been important clients of the Dutch potteries at an early date, which probably explains why it was two Dutchmen (Daniel Behagel and his brother-in-law, Jacobus van de Walle) who founded a factory at Hanau, in 1661. That factory passed through several hands but long retained the marks of its origin: dark outlining (*trek*) was practised, and Chinese forms were in favour. Many blue-and-white pieces from Hanau are so close to their Delft models that there has often been confusion in attributing them. The factories of Heusenstamm and Frankfurt-am-Main imitated delftware, if possible even more closely. A very precise knowledge of the highly homogeneous cobalt-blue delftware is necessary to be able to distinguish the blue wares of the German factories from it. The German ware is generally lighter and less evenly spread.

Historical as well as commercial links between the Netherlands and England were such that the role of delftware was even more preponderant there than elsewhere. In England, delftware, or delft, is synonymous with faience, a term used there only lately as it is in the rest of Europe. From the sixteenth century, as we saw, potters came to work in England from the Netherlands, among them Jasper Andries from Antwerp. Arthur Lane, in *Cahiers de la céramique et des arts du feu*: writes: 'at the beginning, faience making in England and Holland was like two branches of the same school; despite the appearance of some typically English pieces about 1650, the general similarity persisted even in the eighteenth century. The English continued to import Dutch pottery, Dutch potters and even a Dutch king, William III....'

An important event in the history of English ceramics was the arrival at Lambeth of a Dutch potter from Delft, John Ariens van Hamme, who came to 'manufacture tiles and "porcelain" in the manner practised in Holland....' Other Dutch potters came to work in England in the late seventeenth century. Despite the establishment of these factories, England was to rank among the largest clients of Delft. The market seems to follow, more or less, the political relations of the two countries. (Between 1689 and 1702 they shared the same sovereign.) Some commissions are famous, such as that for Hampton Court from Queen Mary, and, probably in its train, those of great English nobles. The admirable article by Arthur Lane on Daniel Marot states how many courtiers commissioned tulip vases. In 1694, William Cavendish, first Duke of Devonshire, ordered forty pagoda vases for Chatsworth, together with a set of eight urns and a two-handled vase. Many of these pieces are marked A.K. William Blathwayt too, the War Minister, ordered a set of tulip vases and urns, marked A.K., for his country house at Dyrham in Gloucestershire. (It is interesting that the architect William Talman, Comptroller of Works at Hampton Court, was involved in furnishing both these houses.) Then there is the tulip vase preserved in the Victoria and Albert Museum, which bears the arms of John Churchill, Duke of Marlborough. It was probably made at the time of the building of Blenheim Palace. The composition of the arms shows that he was already a Prince of the Empire, proving that the piece could not have been made before 1704, the year when Churchill received the title. (This is one of the proofs that the mark A.K. was still used in the first years of the eighteenth century.) The frequent presence of the arms of Great Britain, particularly on Delft *doré*, bears witness to the permanence of Delft's influence in that country.

France too appreciated delftware, and it is usual to quote as proof of the role played by Dutch wares the argument put forward by the famous Rouen faience potter, Louis Poterat, in support of his application for a royal privilege. Poterat intended to manufacture 'a purple faience painted with white and with blue and other colours in the manner of Holland'. The Nevers potters, though their past was impregnated with Italian taste, which was transformed gradually into something more specifically French, nonetheless adopted the Far Eastern style. Here, however, it is difficult to distinguish how far delftware exercised an influence on the Nevers designs in blue-and-white with Chinese scenes, because many pieces are dated quite early. It is only natural that the faience factories at Lille should reflect Delft influence much more strongly. The lightness, brilliance of surface and quality of the cobalt means that some prudence is required in discriminating between the two wares.

There were certainly considerable numbers of Dutch workpeople in many of the French factories, especially in the north of the country. Imports must have been on almost as large a scale in France as in England. One of the earliest importers was the celebrated Claude Révérend. It is known, for example, that a large proportion of the porcelain ornaments for the Trianon at Versailles came from Holland. Révérend is regarded by many scholars as the great supplier of delftware to France. He is typical of a class of merchants that grew rapidly under the policies of Colbert and Louis XIV in the second half of the seventeenth century. Révérend's main profession (salterer) would not seem to have destined him to make faience. In 1659 he was still negotiating sales of fish, but he disappeared in October of that year and did not reappear until 1661. We imagine that first contacts were made in Holland. In April, 1662, we find him at Delft, where he settles an account of 485 florins for delivery of faience with Dirck Hieronymus van Dessel, proprietor of the Peacock factory. Révérend seems to have remained mainly in touch with this factory. However, in 1664, he obtained from the French king an exclusive privilege to 'manufacture faience and counterfeit porcelain in Indian style and to import and sell the faience that he has made and manufactured in Holland'. Despite continuing his fish trade, financial difficulties set in, though this did not prevent Révérend from making some enormous purchases from the Peacock factory in 1665. Since January 1663, this had been in the possession of Wouter van Eenhoorn, Gÿsbrecht Cruych and Willem Cleffius. These links were certainly quite regular, and it can be seen from declarations by the workers that Révérend was closely observing and studying the methods of faience manufacture. It became more and more difficult to make payments. While undertaking the installation of a factory at Saint Cloud with his brother's help, Révérend placed merchandise in bond with Van Reijgersbergen, faience potter at Delft, which was seized when the latter went bankrupt. In 1666, Claude Révérend, faced with bankruptcy himself, handed over the factory of Saint Cloud (where Dutch workpeople were very probably employed) to his brother François. François supplied many vases and tiles to Versailles, as shown in the accounts of the King's Works.

The activity of the Révérend brothers continued until about 1680. This fact is very important, because it rules out the hypothesis—too often advanced in former years—that the Révérend family played a fundamental part in the long history of the sale of delftware in France. From the beginning of the eighteenth century, all the ware that can be identified as being indisputably made for France represents a quite different chapter in the history of the trade with Holland. It is in this context that the French taste for Delft *doré* in the style of East India Company wares belongs. In this category are plates with the arms of several of the great French courtiers.

CONCLUSION

We would ask the reader to leaf through these pages once more, to try to list all the characteristics, the variety of inspiration, the faithful reflection of the spirit of a people and the many technical inventions that make up delftware. He will then surely be filled with wonder and respect for the incredible creative power of those potters who for some 150 years made an outstanding contribution to the history of European faience.

The end of the eighteenth century saw a recession, in both quality and quantity, in the production of delftware. The few designs still current were treated in a simplified manner, almost mechanically. From the middle of the eighteenth century, we have seen that enamelling was abandoned, probably because of the high cost of production and because of the competition from the French ceramic production then in its heyday. Subsequently, delftware went into competition with European porcelain, which was becoming more and more common. Finally, just like France, Holland was unable to stand up to the invasion of English 'cream ware', which was expanding enormously. 'Cream ware' was particularly well suited to industrial manufacture, so it was low in cost and perfectly adapted to the creation of the neo-classical objects fashion required. When this invasion took place at the end of the eighteenth century, there was no alternative for craftsman-made wares of tin-glazed earthenware but to go under.

In this historical context, the inventive commercial spirit of the English brought into existence a very original production: 'English delft'. This cream-coloured ware is not to be confused with 'delftware', that is tin-glazed faience made in England in the style of faience from Delft.

John Turner (the equal of Wedgwood, says Honey in *European Ceramic Art*), a great English potter at Stoke-on-Trent, manufacturer of cream-coloured ware and stoneware, installed himself in 1762 at Lane End in Staffordshire. Turner's affairs prospered, and he conceived the idea of devoting a section of his activities to manufacturing products for Holland. He set up a depot in Delft. Some writers think that Turner installed decorating workshops there too and that a whole series of pieces came from these workshops: some with biblical scenes or domestic interiors, others with Orangist propaganda and

Pl. 180

---

180 Two plates and a saucer: fine English faience of the type called 'English delftware', (top left) mark (in hollow relief) TURNER, late 18th or early 19th century. Plates: D. 24 cm, saucer: D. 18 cm. Musée national de Céramique, Sèvres: plates, inv. 4204, 4740; saucer, inv. 5955, Dagneau Donation.

Pieces of English manufacture in cream-coloured ware are well known. They were made for export to Holland in the late eighteenth and early nineteenth centuries. Plates illustrating the story of the Prodigal Son are often found. Here are two episodes from this Bible story with inscriptions describing the scene: (top right) ZYN AFSCHEID (his departure) and (top left) ZYN ARREMOE (his poverty). According to Donald Turner in *Creamware,* the decoration is borrowed from engravings by John Aynsley. The plate at the top right bears the hollow mark of Turner, a very important Staffordshire potter. Some writers suppose that these pieces, manufactured in England, might have been decorated at Delft. The rather crude vivid colours, red, yellow, green, blue and black, are a result of the nature of the support. Other types of decoration are found in the same style: religious subjects, boats, domestic scenes and, above all, patriotic subjects.

The saucer depicts the busts of William V of Orange and Princess Frederick Sophie Wilhelmine, as indicated by the initials; they are separated by an orange tree. Below them is an inscription to the glory of the sovereigns. The piece celebrates the return from exile of the royal pair in 1787.

180

185

some with seascapes (dishes perhaps for ships). Most of the pieces have inscriptions in Dutch.

In 1765, the Scot MacPherson noted in the trade annals that the English used to eat their meals from dishes made at Delft in Holland; however, when he wrote, the Dutch were using English pottery from Staffordshire. From 1760 onwards, English exports of Staffordshire pottery to Holland were really astonishing.

But the production of true delftware was not yet at an end. Here are the names of a few of the last potters: the best known was Henricus Arnoldus Piccardt, a strange individual who found himself deprived of his captaincy at the proclamation of the Batavian Republic because he was an Orangist; Piccardt thereupon took over the direction of the old Porcelain Bottle factory, so that he was able to carry on propaganda for his protectors. This enterprise enjoyed the participation of some Englishmen, among them Adolf Tulk.

We have already described the sorry end of the lovely Dutch craft of making delftware. Gerrit Paape wrote in 1794: 'In our country where they seem keener on making money than on giving the arts and sciences all the scope they can enjoy, they soon ceased to bring to the justly famous decoration of our faiences the same care as in the past, and the quality declined at the same time as its external beauty...the masters found themselves constrained either to lower quality or to raise prices.'

It would be unjust, however, to pass over the way in which Holland reacted—like all the other countries of Europe—to the loss of the prestige of faience. She went in for the art of porcelain.

Dutch porcelain is too often neglected. It deserves mention, even though it only appeared at a relatively late date. The products from Weesp go back to about 1764 and soon after came those of Oude Loosdrecht and Amstel, while the ceramic history of The Hague is far from being uninteresting. A faience factory had been established at The Hague in the seventeenth century by two Dutchmen. Porcelain manufacture began about 1773, probably starting simply as a painting workshop.

While these diverse activities, corresponding to the development of taste and fashion, are of undoubted interest in the history of Dutch pottery, it remains true that for most connoisseurs it is delftware that is rightly regarded as the finest flower of the potter's art in the Netherlands.

FACTORY MARKS

The Three Golden Ash Barrels
(*De 3 Vergulde Astonnekens*)

1   Gerrit Pietersz Kam, *c.* 1680-1705

Z·DEX

2   Zacharias Dextra, *c.* 1712-62

3   Late eighteenth century

The Golden Flowerpot (*De Vergulde Bloempot*)

4   Second half of eighteenth century

5   Second half of eighteenth century

The Golden Boat (*De Vergulde Boot*)

D. VK boot
1700

6   Dirck van der Kest, 1698-1701

IDA

7   Johan den Appel, *c.* 1760.

The Porcelain Axe (*De Porceleyne Bijl*)

8   Late eighteenth century

9   Late eighteenth century

10   Hugo Justusz Brouwer, *c.* 1780

The Porcelain Claw (*De Porceleyne Claeuw*)

11   1705-70

12   1705-70

13   1705-70

The Porcelain Bottle (*De Porceleyne Fles*)

14   Pieter van Doorne, *c.* 1765

15   Jacubus Harlees, *c.* 1770-85

The Fortune (*T'Fortuyn*)

16   Late seventeenth century

17   Joris Mesch, 1706-30 (?)

18   Van den Briel, *c.* 1760

The Greek A (*De Grieksche A*)

19, 20, 21   Samuel van Eenhoorn, 1674-86

188

22, 23   Adriaen Kocks, late seventeenth century and early eighteenth

24, 25, 26   Pieter Adriaensz Kocks, mark continued after his death, first quarter of eighteenth century

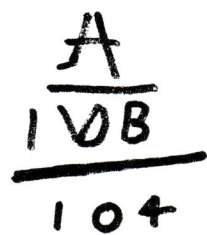

27   Van den Briel, late eighteenth century

28   Jacobus Adriaensz Halder, late eighteenth century

29   Jan Theunis Dextra, late eighteenth century

The Heart (*T'Hart*)

30, 31   Jan van der Laan, late seventeenth century

The Three Bells (*De 3 Klokken*)

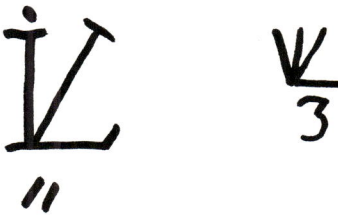

32, 33   Jansz van der Laan, late seventeenth century

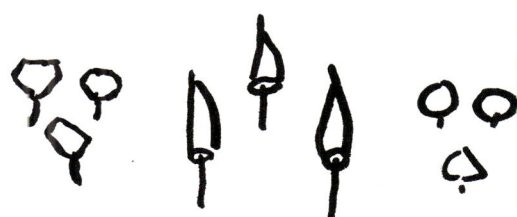

34, 35, 36   Eighteenth century

The Porcelain Ewer (*De Porceleyn Lampetkan*)

37, 38   1723-80

The Young Moor's Head (*Het Jonge Moriaenshooft*)

39, 40   Jacob Wemmersz Hoppesteyn, marks continued after his death from the late seventeenth century to the early eighteenth

41 Rochus Jacobsz Hoppesteyn, 1679-92

LvD

42 Mark attributed to Lieven van Dalen, c. 1692-1730

jvH

43 Mark attributed to Jan van der Hagen

The Old Moor's Head (*Het Oude Moriaenshooft*)

44 Late seventeenth century and early eighteenth

45 Geertruy Verstelle, c. 1760

The Peacock (*De Paauw*)

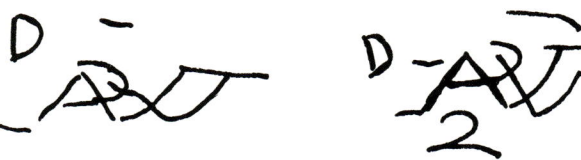

46, 47 Eighteenth century

IVH

48 Johannes ver Hagen, 1730

The Metal Pot (*De Metalen Pot*)

49 Lambertus Cleffius, late seventeenth century

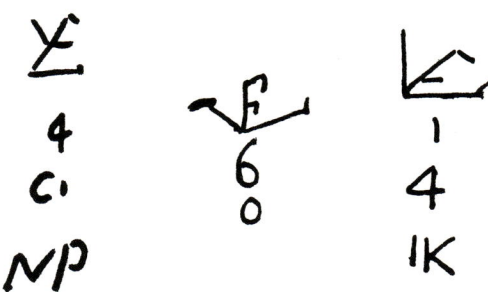

50, 51, 52 Lambertus van Eenhoorn, 1691-1721

53 Jan van der Wall, late seventeenth century

The Roman (*De Romeyn*)

P.V.M.   PM

54, 55   Petrus van Marum, 1754-64

56   Jan van der Kloot, 1764

The Rose (*De Roos*)

Roos

57   Early eighteenth century

R

58   Early eighteenth century

59   Mark attributed to the Rose factory

60   Eighteenth century

C V Dyk
in de roos

61   Cornelis van Dyk, 1739-55

62, 63   Dirck van der Does, 1755-70

The Two Ships (*De Twee Scheepjes*)

K

64   Mark attributed by some to Cornelis Aelbrechtsz Keyser, late seventeenth century

iG
32

65   Jan Gaal, 1707-25

66, 67   Anthony Pennis, 1759-70

The Double Tankard (*De Dobbelde Schenckan*)

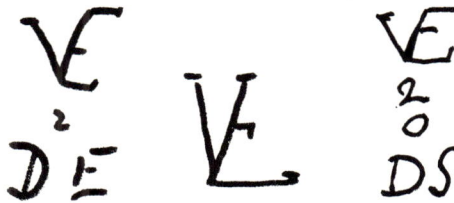

68, 69, 70   Louwÿs Victorsz, early eighteenth century

(There is no way of distinguishing the marks of Louwÿs Victorsz and Lambertus van Eenhoorn.)

191

71 Mark noted as having been registered by the factory in 1764

The Porcelain Dish (*De Porceleyne Schotel*)

72 Gÿsbrecht Lambrechtsz Gruyck, late seventeenth century. (This mark has been variously attributed.)

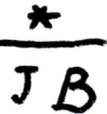

73 Johannes van Duyn, 1764-77

The White Star (*De Witte Starre*)

74 Lambertus Cleffius, late seventeenth century

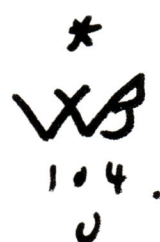

75 Dirck Witsemburgh, late seventeenth century

76 Albertus Kiell, late eighteenth century

77 Cornelis Dircksz de Berg, late eighteenth century

78 Johannes de Aerg, late eighteenth century

The Two Wild Men (*De Twee Wildemannen*)

79 Willem van Beek, late eighteenth century

Factories Producing Red Stoneware

80, 81 Ary-Jansz de Milde (mark on seal), *c.* 1680-1708

82 Mark on seal, attributed to Ary-Jansz de Milde, *c.* 1680-1708

83, 84   Jacobus de Caluwe (mark on seal), 1708-30

Unidentified Marks

85, 86, 87, 88   Unidentified marks, mostly on pieces of Delft *doré*, often of great quality, and on pieces with high-temperature polychrome decoration and French inscriptions, early eighteenth century

Rié

Réinier

89   Undeciphered signature, late seventeenth century, only known on an oval plaque in the Musée national de Céramique, Sèvres

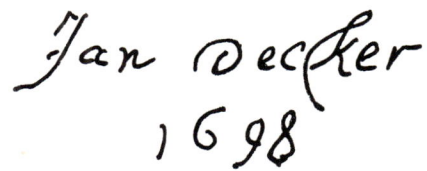

90   Undeciphered signature, late seventeenth century

J·BAAM

91   Unknown name, perhaps that of the owner of the piece (see Pl. 120), late eighteenth century

TOME
& WA

92   Mark found on a famous dish in the Rijksmuseum, depicting the Last Judgement in blue-and-white with a few touches of colour

·H·V·E·

93   Mark found on a plaque in the Musée national Adrien Dubouché, Limoges

Jan Decker
1698

94   Signature on a bust in the Musées royaux d'Art et d'Histoire, Brussels

1634
DEN 2 M

95   Signature of the monogrammist C.H. on the Battle of Vught dish (Pl. 7), which has been variously interpreted

Y   VA

96, 97   These marks appear mainly on a special type of butter dish of shell shape; a number are known in museum and private collections.

Factories outside Delft

98, 99 Arnhem factory, 1755-73

C:BOVMEESTER

C:BM

100, 101 Rotterdam factory: Cornelis Boumeester, 1675-1700, generally in seascape panels on a barrel or a piece of flotsam

102 Rotterdam monogram, late eighteenth century

103, 104 Makkum factory marks that can be attributed to the factory there, late eighteenth century

BIBLIOGRAPHY

Old Editions

Bleyxwijck, D. Van. *Beschrijvinge der Stadt Delft*. Delft, 1667; 1680.
Boitet, R. *Beschrijvinge der Stadt Delft*. Delft, 1729.
Paape, Gerrit. *De Plateelbakker of Delftsch Aardewerk Maaker*. Dordrecht, 1794.
Passe, Crispijn van de. *Hortus Floridus 1614: Nederlandsche Vertaling van 1614: Den Bloemhof*. Arnhem, 1614.

Specialized Works

Blümlein, C. *Delft und seine Fayencen*. Hamburg, 1899.
Danis, Robert. *La première maison royale de Trianon*. Paris, 1926.
Fourest, H.P. *Les Faïences de Delft*. Paris, 1957.
Garner, F.H. and Michael Archer. *English Delftware*. 2nd rev. ed., London, 1972.
Havard, Henry. *Catalogue des faïences de Delft, composant la collection de Mr John Loudon*. The Hague, 1874.
—. *Histoire de la faïence de Delft*. Paris, 1878.
Honey, W.B. *European Ceramic Art*. 2 vols., London, 1952.
Hoynck van Papendrecht, A.H.H. *De Rotterdamsche Plateel'en Tegelbakkers en hun Product 1590-1851*. Rotterdam, 1920.
Hudig, Ferrand W. *Delfter Fayence*. Berlin, 1929.
Imber, D. *Collecting Delft*. London, 1968.
Jonge, C.H. de. *Delft Ceramics*. (Trans. by Marie Christine Hellin) New York, Washington, D.C., London, 1970.
Justice, Jean. *Dictionnaire des marques et monogrammes de la faïence de Delft*. Paris, Brussels, 1920.
Kjellberg, Sven T. *Fajanfund i Göteborg Sätryck ur Göteborgs Musei*. Arstryck, 1933.
Lane, Arthur. *A Guide to Tiles*. 2nd ed. London, 1960.
Lion-Goldschmidt, Daisy. *Les poteries et porcelaines chinoises*. Paris, 1957.
Lunsingh Scheurleer, T.H. *Wik Delfts*. Lochem, de Tijdstroom, 1970.
—. *Delfts blauw*. Bussum, 1975.
Mariën-Dugardin, A.M. *Une cruche en faïence de Delft: A l'occasion d'une exposition organisée aux Musées Royaux d'Art et d'Histoire*. Brussels, 1971.
Neurdenburg, E. 'De Pladeelbakkers-familie Hoppesteyn' in *Feestbundel Dr. A. Bredius*. Amsterdam, 1915, p. 191.
—. 'Oude Aardewerk toegelicht aan de verzamelingen' in *Het Nederlandsch Museum voor Geschredenis en Kunst te Amsterdam*, 2nd ed. Amsterdam, 1920, pp. 181-97.
—. *Delftsch Aardewerk*, n.p. 1943.
— and B. Rackham. *Old Dutch Pottery and Tiles*. London, 1923.
Noothoven van Goor, J.M. *De Arnhemse Aardewerk-fabriek*. Amsterdam, 1954.
Ottema, N. *Friesche Majolica*. Leeuwarden, 1920.
Rackham, Bernard. *Early Netherlands' Majolica*. London, 1926.
— and A. Van der Put. *The Three Books of the Potter's Art by Cipriano Piccolpasso*. London, 1934.
Turner, Donald. *Creamware*. London, 1978.
Vecht, A. *Frederik van Frijtom*. Amsterdam, 1968.
Weigert, Roger-Armand. *Le style Louis XIV*. Paris, 1941.
Wittop-Koning, D.A. *Delftse Apothekers-potten*. Deventer, 1954.

Articles:

Archer, Michael. 'Pyramids and Pagodas for Flowers,' in *Country Life*. London, 22 January, 1976, pp. 166-9.
Birkenmager, E. 'La Décoration peinte des garnitures polychromes de la Faïencerie "De metalen Pot" appartenant aux collections Wilanow, Delft vers 1710,' in *Bulletin du Musée National de Varsovie*. XII, Warsaw, 1971, pp. 65-7.
Blaaunen, A. L. den. 'Ceramik met Chinoiserieën naar prenten van Petrus Schenk FJr,' in *Bulletin van het Rijksmuseum*. II, Amsterdam 1964, pp. 35-49.
Gelder, H.E. van. 'L'obélisque en majolique de Delft,' in *Faenza*. IV, Faenza, 1950, pp. 77-8.
—. 'Het Grote tegel tableau des Collectie Loudon,' in *Bulletin van het Rijksmuseum*. IV, Amsterdam, 1956, p. 96.
—. 'La majolique de Delft et ses marques,' in *Faenza*. V; VI, Faenza, 1959, pp. 116-19.
Hambis, L. 'Une plaque de Delft conservée au Musée Lecuyer de Saint Quentin,' in *Arts Asiatiques*. XIX, Paris, 1969, pp. 169-73.
Helbig, J. 'La Salle Evenepoël aux Musées Royaux d'Art et d'Histoire de Bruxelles,' in *Faenza*. II, Faenza, 1959, pp. 27-9.
Heukensfeldt-Jansen, M.A. 'Een Spiegellijst van polychrom Delfts aardewerk nit het eerste kwart van XVIIIe eeuw,' in *Bulletin van het Rijksmuseum*. VII, Amsterdam, 1959, pp. 74-5.
—. 'Een Koelvat met twe blessen van polychrom Delfts aardewerk nit het eerste kwart van XVIIIe eeuw,' in *Bulletin van het Rijksmuseum*. VII, Amsterdam, 1959, pp. 76-7.
Hudig, Ferrand W. 'Delftica,' in *Oud-Holland*. Amsterdam, 1929, p. 53.
Jestaz, B. 'Les modèles de la majolique historiée: XVIIe et XVIIIe siècles,' in *Gazette des Beaux-Arts*. no. 81, Paris, 1973, pp. 109-20.

Jonge, C.H. de. 'Delftware at Vught: The Fentener van Vlissingen Collection,' in *Apollo*, LXXX, London, 1964, pp. 384-9.

—. 'Delfter Keramik aus dem Niederland übers Tübingen: Wasmut 1969,' (review by J. Mallet) in *Burlington Magazine*. CXIII, London 1971, p. 479.

Lane, Arthur. 'Daniel Marot, Designer of Delft Vases and of Gardens at Hampton Court,' in *The Connoisseur*. London, March, 1949, pp. 19-24

—. 'English delftware' in *Cahiers de la céramique et des arts du feu*. No. 6, Paris, 1957, pp. 74-88.

—. 'Delftse Tegels mit Hampton Court en Daniel Marot's Werkzaamhied aldaar,' in *Bulletin van het Rijksmuseum*. VII, Amsterdam, 1959, pp. 12-21.

Leeuw, R.A. 'Rijksmuseum "Huis Lambert van Meerten" te Delft,' in *Nederlandse Rijksmusea*. XCV, S' Gravenhage, 1973, pp. 191-4.

—. idem, XCVI, S' Gravenhage, 1974, pp. 137-9.

Lunsingh Sheurleer, T.H. 'Collectie M.G. van Heel oud Delfts Aardewerk: Rijksmuseum Twenthe, Enschede,' in *Medbl Vrienden nederlandsche Ceramick*. S' Gravenhage, 1969, p. 76.

—. 'Orange Ceramick in het Kominklijk Huisar chief te S' Gravenhage,' in *Nederlandsche Kunsthistorisch-jaarboek*. XXI, Amsterdam, 1970, pp. 243-6.

—. 'Opneen eendecor met twee papagauien en een versiering van bloemenmanden,' in *Antiek*. VIII, Lochem, 1973, pp. 234-41.

—. 'Demftse Wapenborden mit het eerste Kwart van de achttiende eeuw,' in *Antiek*. VI, Lochem, 1973, pp. 563-9.

Mala, D. 'Delftský fajans ve státním Musen v. Mnichově Hradisti,' in *Spr. Pamakt Pěč*. XVII, Prague, 1957, pp. 139-47.

Mariën-Dugardin, A.M. 'Une paire de vaches en faïence de Delft,' in *Bulletin des Musées Royaux d'Art et d'Histoire*. XXXIII, Brussels, 1961, pp. 70-2.

—. 'Delfts aardewerk met gekleurd fond v. 1675-1730,' in *Antiek*. VI, Lochem, 1971-2, pp. 100-12.

Mikhajlova, O. 'Igdelija Samuelaja van Enkhoorna va Sobranii Ermitaža,' in *Soobščenija Gosudarstvennogo Ordena Lenina Ermitaža*. XIV, Leningrad, 1958, pp. 40-2.

—. 'Bljudo del'ftakogo fajansa S. monogramma AR,' in *Soobščenija Gosudarstvennogo Ordena Lenina Ermitaža*. XVI, Leningrad, 1959, pp. 40-1.

—. 'K raparozu o vozniknovanii v delfte fajansov s rosfis'ju, padražajušči Kitajskmu parforu,' in *Soobščenija Gosudarstvennogo Ordena Lenina Ermitaža*. XIX, Leningrad, 1960, pp. 19-23.

—. 'K voprosu o polikhromnau Del'fte t.n. mufelnogo obžiga,' in *Soobščenija Gosudarstvennogo Ordena Lenina Ermitaža*. XXVIII, Leningrad, 1967, pp. 29-32.

—. 'Gollauskae bljudo s gerbom stroganovgkn,' in *Soobščenija Gosudarstvennogo Ordena Lenina Ermitaža*. XXX, Leningrad, 1969, pp. 18-20.

Neurdenburg, E. 'Net Adriaen Pijnacker maar Pieter: Adriaensz Kocx en diens weduwe' in De Grieksche A' te Delft,' in *Oudherkundig Jaarboek*. XII n.p., 1943, pp. 31 ff.

Nicaise, H. 'Bijdrage tot een Nederlandsche terminologie omtrent oude ceramickkunst' in *Kunst* DLV (Amsterdam, 1934).

—. 'Zuidnederlandsche Majolika-fabrieken uit de XVIe eeuw' in *Oud-Holland*. Amsterdam, 1936, p. 201.

—. 'Les modèles italiens des faïences néerlandais au XVIe et au début du XVIIe siècle,' in *Bulletin de l'Institut historique belge à Rome*. XIII, Rome, 1936, p. 109.

Peelen, Ida C.E. 'Tegeltableaux uit het midden der XVIIe eeuw,' in *Bulletin van den Nederlandschen Oudherkundigen Bond*. Leiden, 1920, p. 215.

—. 'Versiernigen optegels naar ontwerfen van Daniel Marot,' in *Oudherkundig Jaarboek*. N.p., 1920, p. 160.

Romijn, J. 'Un violon et une cafetière XVIIIe siècle,' in *Vrienden van de nederlandse Ceramick Amsterdam*. No. 51, Amsterdam, 1967, p. 26.

Schaap, E. 'Three Delft Pieces in the Philadelphia Museum of Art,' in *Bulletin of the Philadelphia Museum of Art*. LXII, Philadelphia, 1966-7, pp. 276-91.

Skov, S. 'En isbjørnetallerken fa Delft,' in *Handels-og Søfartmuseet Kronburg Arl*. Helsingør, 1966, pp. 261-6.

Tait, H. 'Delft Preacher's Plate,' in *Apollo*. LVI, London, 1962, pp. 620-1.

Tazanova, E. 'Les assiettes du Couronnement fabriquées à Delft: 1712,' in *Zbornik Slovenskeo Narodnekp Muzea Historia*. Bratislava, n.d.

Thaman, H.E. 'Die "Delftse Pottenkamer" der J.R. Geigy A.G., Basel,' in *Keramikfreunde der Schweiz*. No. 65, Basle, 1964, pp. 3-15.

Vecht, A. 'Faïences primitives des Pays-Bas du Nord,' in *Cahiers de la Céramique et des Arts du feu*. No. 2, Paris, 1956, pp. 17-32.

Visser, M.A. de. 'Roode Steenen trekpotjes met het werk Arij de Milde,' in *Oudherkundig Jaarboek*. VII n.p., 1928, p. 99.

—. 'Roode Delftsche theepotten van Lambert van Eenhoorn en van de Rotte in het Groningen Museum,' in *Oud-Holland*. LXXII, Amsterdam, 1957, pp. 104-10.

Westers, A. 'Een Snockenterrine van Delfts aardewerk,' in *Bulletin du Musée Boymans van Beuningen*. XI, Rotterdam, 1960, pp. 62-8.

—. 'Een lampetkan van Delfts aardewerk,' in *Bulletin du Musée Boymans van Beuningen*. XII, Rotterdam, 1961, pp. 88-97.

Witteveen, A. 'Tabak en Tabakshandel ap Delftse Borden,' in *Antiek*. VIII, no. 4, Lochem, 1973, pp. 298-305.

Exhibitions:

Gemeentemuseum van S'. Gravenhage: *Tentoonstelling Nederlands Aardewerk 1500-1800*, S' Gravenhage, 1949.

Helbig, J. *Faïences hollandaises*. (Exhibition catalogue). Musées royaux d'Art et d'Histoire, Brussels, n.d.

Heukensfeldt-Jansen, M.A. *Delfts Aardewerk*, (Exhibition catalogue). Rijksmuseum, Amsterdam, 1955.

Jansen, B. *Chinese invloeden of polychroom Delfts Aardewerk: de Hoppesteyns*. (Exhibition catalogue). Gemeentemuseum, S', Gravenhage, 1955.

—. *Gleyersgoet en Delfts blauw*. (Exhibition catalogue). Gemeentemuseum, S.' Gravenhage, 1958.

Peelen, Ida C.E. *Catalogus van de kerzameling Nederlandsch Aardewerk*. (Exhibition Catalogue). Gemeentemuseum, S.' Gravenhage, 1917.

Skov, S. *Delft Fayencer pa Koldinghees*. (Exhibition catalogue). Kolding museet, Kolding, 1962.

Voskuil-Groenewegen, S.M. *Gekleurd Delfts Aardewerk*. (Exhibition catalogue). Gemeente Museum, The Hague, 1969.

—. *Nederlandse Tegel ca. 1600-1800*. (Exhibition catalogue). Gemeente Museum, The Hague, 1974.

PHOTO CREDITS

The numbers refer to plate numbers. The photographs were provided by:

Amsterdam, Rijksmuseum   9, 10, 13, 14, 16, 22-24, 37, 41, 42, 58, 74, 83, 84, 86, 101, 112, 114, 116, 129, 139, 161, 176

Brussels, Musées Royaux d'Art et d'Histoire   7, 8, 12, 39, 59, 97, 156, 160, 167, 168, 179 (photos: A.C.L., Brussels); 47, 69, 100, 133, 136 (photos: Speltdoorn, Brussels)

Delft, Stedelijk Museum «Het Prinsenhof» 57, 95 (photos: A. Dingjan, The Hague)

Douai, Musée Municipal   36

Hampton Court Palace   26 (photo: Lord Chamberlain's Office, London); 27, 28 (photos: Property Services Agency, London)

The Hague, Gemeente Museum   19, 31, 50, 51, 61, 62, 71, 78, 104, 138, 140, 157, 159

Lille, Musée des Beaux-Arts   102, 107

Limoges, Musée National Adrien Dubouché   21, 33, 49, 66-68, 90, 105, 146, 154, 162, 166, 177 (photos: Georges Routhier, Paris)

London, British Museum   34, 40, 53, 119, 163

London, Victoria and Albert Museum   25, 30, 44, 63, 73, 76, 81, 93

Paris, Musée des Arts Décoratifs   32, 64, 72, 79, 87, 91, 115, 117, 123, 127, 132, 137, 142, 144, 147, 149, 151, 153, 169, 173, 170 (photos: Musée des Arts Décoratifs, Laurent Sully Jaulmes, Paris)

Paris, Musée Carnavalet   121 (photo: Georges Routhier, Paris)

Paris, Musée du Conservatoire National de Musique   164 (photo: Georges Routhier, Paris)

Rouen, Musée des Beaux-Arts   11, 165 (photo: Ellebé, Rouen)

Sèvres, Musée National de Céramique   1-6, 15, 17, 18, 20, 29, 35, 43, 45, 46, 48, 52, 54-56, 60, 65, 70, 75, 80, 82, 96, 98, 106, 108, 109, 118, 120, 122, 125, 126, 128, 130, 131, 134, 135, 143, 145, 148, 150, 152, 174, 178, 180 (photos: Georges Routhier, Paris); 38, 77, 94, 176 (photos: Michel Nahmias, Paris); 113 (photo: des Musées Nationaux, Paris)

The following photographs were taken by Georges Routhier, Paris: 85, 88, 89, 92, 99, 103, 110, 111, 124, 141, 155, 158, 171, 172

INDEX

The numbers in italics refer to plate numbers.

Abrahams, Gérald 7
Aix-la-Chapelle, Treaty of 19
Albissola 9
Amsterdam 9, 19, 20
Andries, Jasper 182
   Joris 9
angels *152*
   cherubs 74
   cupids 22, *137*
      frieze of *7*
   putti 10
      frieze of *21*
      in reserve *20*
      playing trumpets *40*
animals 24, *28*
   bat *150*
   birds, *4, 11, 21, 24, 51, 72, 73, 75, 86, 98*
   beaks *81*
   cocks *75, 155*
   ducks *76*
   eagles *109*
   fanciful *105*
   heron *95*
   parrots *81, 106, 160*
   peacocks *150, 151*
   perching *57, 72, 79, 94, 117*
   plover *155*
   poultry *155*
   boar *155*
      leaping *157*
   butterflies *86, 114*
   cows *155*
      pair of *161*
   deer 10, *128, 155*
   dogs *157*
   hare *4*
   hind *150*
   horse *98, 155*
   imaginary: *see* dragons, phoenixes, unicorns
   insects 10, *98*
   leopard *75, 85, 94*
   snake *15*
   stag *123, 155*
Anspach 17
Anstett, Nicolas 186
antimony 17, 18; *see also* yellow
Antwerp 5, 9
   workshops of *176*
Archer, Michael 25, *55*
Arita 75
'Armenian bol': *see* red slip
armorial devices 10, *67, 69, 72, 74, 98, 109, 110*
   Frederick I, King of Prussia 76, *109*
   George I, King of England 76
   Louis Alexandre of Bourbon 76, *109*
   Nicolas Auguste de la Baume 76, *109*
   Van der Hoeve family 156
Arosa 7
Arouwer, Justus *121*
assiettes parlantes 73
Autumn 26

bands *84*
   broad *37*
   eight-sided *71*
   straight *123*
Bartoli, Pietro Santo 24
base *73, 77*
   octagonal *37,* 40
   truncated 26
basins
   basket-shaped *74*
   footed 26
   lidded 76
   oval *80*
   system of 17
baskets
   of flowers *75, 121*
   of fruit 22, *123*
   openwork 26, *51, 59*
beakers
   octagonal 26
   round 26
Behagel, Daniel 182
Belgium 7
Bérain, Jean and Claude 22
Bergh, Cornelis van den *125*
   Johannes de 70
Berghem, Van 10, *130*
biblical subjects 10, 23; *see also* Christ
birds: *see* animals
biscuit wares 75; *see also* firing
black 17, 74, *88-9, 112*
   manganese- *49*
   touches of *81, 84*; *see also trek*
Blacks: *see* Negroes
blanc de Chine 24
bleu d'empois: *see* grounds
bleu persan: *see* grounds
bliksem dekor: *see* 'lightning motif'
blue *1, 3, 4,* 10, *13, 15,* 17, 18, *18,* 19, *21, 21,* 24, *74, 77, 80, 81, 82, 83, 86, 95*
   and green 18
   and red 74
   -and-white decoration *6,* 10, *21-3, 63, 64, 68, 70, 71, 72, 72, 73, 74, 75, 76, 78, 118, 121, 126*
   cobalt 17, 74
   high-fired *111*
   patch of *96*
   strong *31, 32, 71*
   tones of *14*
   turquoise *110*
   underglaze 75
body
   fluted *83*
   heart-shaped *103*
Bogaert, Adriaen 9
   Jan 9
bolus: *see* red slip
bottles *16,* 24, *74, 79, 103,* 110
   beaker-shaped 26
   booted *74*
   faceted *61*
   handled *37*
Boumeester, Cornelis *174, 176*

bouquet *90*
bowls 10, 24, 76
   barber's *123*
   bulb *103*
   cream *45*
   fruit *3,* 19
   octagonal 25
   salad 20
   strawberry *133*
boxes
   cylindrical *138*
   lidded *138*
   money *110, 132*
   oval *155*
   rectangular 26
   spice *15,* 22
   tobacco *155*
brackets *72*
braid
   blue *126*
   latticed *112*
branches
   flowering *19, 25, 96, 128*
   network of *30*
   olive *67*
   scatter of *73*
Bréauté, Sire de 7
Breugel 8
Bril, Paul 9
'brocaded' decoration 75
Brouwer, Justus 122
brown *1,* 24, *113*
Bruges 9
brush
   holders *127*
   pot 20
buckets *155*
Burgh, A.H.H. van der 7
bushes *31*
   flowering *74, 104*
Bruyelles 17

cage, bird *123, 171*
Caluwe, Jacobus de 25
candlesticks 26, *123, 145*
Caravaggio, Polidoro da 24, *40*
cartouches *2, 21, 37, 64, 68, 86, 120*
   fleur-de-lis *26*
   harp *26*
   heart-shaped *44*
   in reserve *37, 121*
   rococo *140*
   thistle *26*
   waterlily-shaped *123*
'cashmere' motif 74
Cassius, purple of: *see* red from gold
Cavendish, William 182
cavetto *2,* 19, *69, 71, 75, 86, 109*
   low *81*
Champfleury 182
Charles V 9
chests *147*
chequer motif *51, 77*
chimeras *18,* 26

frieze of 74
kind of *86*
with huge beak *36*
China/Chinese 10, *15, 17,* 19, 20, 22-5 and *passim*
   fortified city of *35*
   motifs *5, 15, 16, 82*
Christ 51
   life of *13, 67, 115*
cisterns *123, 130*
classicism 19 and *passim*
clay 20
   Delft 17
   fine sandy 18
   kneading of 17
   Rhine 17
   Tournai 17
   washing of 17
   weathering of 17
Cleffius, Lambertus 23, 74
   Willem 74, *77, 122,* 183; *see also* factories
clock faces 170
clouds (Chinese) 17, *23, 30, 36, 86, 96, 98, 122, 150*
Cock, Hieronymus 26, *60*
coffee-pot 76, *95, 123, 142, 144, 179*
Commedia dell'arte *105*
consoles 22
coolers 74, 76
coperta 17
cornices 22
costume, ballet *163*
crown (royal) 17, *26, 27*
   closed 22
   comital *67*
cruets 21
   double 76
Cruych, Gÿsbrecht 183
cupboards 26
   in Dutch houses 26
cups 25
   wine *29*
Cussac 7
cymbals 24

Dalen, Lieven van 75
   Lucas *99*
   Yvan van *99*
Decker, C. *34*
   Jan 156
deities, Chinese *155*
Delft
   breweries 19
   city of 7, 9, 10, 18, 19, 21, 22-3, *105*
   cloth 19
   destruction of (1608) 19
   doré 24, *73, 75-6, 117*
   explosion of powder magazine (1654) 19
   pastors of *33*
   people of *33*
   'peasant' *150 f, 151, 153*
delftware 7, 9, 10, 17, 18 and *passim*
   'English' 7, *180, 184*

198

'French' 65
'golden age' of 88-9
Demmin 70
derle (faience clay): see clay, Tournai
Deruta: see factories
Dextra, Jan Theunis 128, 138
  Zacharias 140
dish
  Battle of Vught 21
  Boucher de Perthes (plate) 122
dishes 1, 2, 3, 4, 5, 9, 12, 13, 17, 18, 20, 20, 21, 21, 22, 23, 38, 40, 48, 65, 66, 67, 68, 70, 71, 72, 75, 75, 81, 82, 87, 90, 106, 109, 115, 116, 121, 123, 125, 126, 135, 136, 137
  broadrimmed 75
  butter 130
  flanged rim 25
  fruit 76
  'playing card' 137
  polygonal 75, 108
  scalloped profile 25
  sets of 120, 121, 121
  Spanish 3
  sweetmeat 25, 41, 42, 43
  'talking' (plates) 73
  without rim 25
Dordrecht 9
dragons 31, 74
draperies 22
  effects of 64
Duke of Devonshire 25
Dutch East India Company 10, 17, 20, 109, 117, 130; see also shareholders

edge, lobed 66
  with hatching 86
Eenhoorn, Judith van 22
  Lambertus van 74, 75, 92, 93, 101, 117, 125
  Samuel van 15, 20, 21, 23, 26, 30, 61
  'style' of 22
  Wouter van 21-2, 183
Eenkhuysen 9
emblems 10, 17, 77, 109
enamels 38, 114
England 19
engraving 2, 10, 11, 13, 21, 22, 23, 26, 28, 30, 33, 38, 62, 121, 135
  by Rubens 38
  Dutch 24, 73
European motifs 26, 38, 40, 67, 73, 74, 78, 81, 82, 87 and passim
Evenepoël, Albert 7; see also museums, Sèvres
ewers 19, 21, 24, 25
  'helmet' 105
  Near Eastern 95
  tray for 19

facets 79
factories 22-3, 74, 93, 117
  Arnhem 180
  Axe 122
  Deruta (Umbria) 1, 10
  Double Tankard 74
  Eenhoorn, Samuel van
    factories of 15, 16
  English 150
  Fortune 134
  Frankfurt-am-Main 182
  French 128
  Frisian 180
  Golden Boat 73
  Greek A 20, 22, 32, 52, 74, 158
  Hanan 182
  Heart 152
  Heusenstamm 182
  Jesuit-run 76
  Jingdezhen 20
  Lambeth 123
  Metal Pot 23, 74
  Old Moor's Head 23, 130
  Peacock 23, 122, 127, 131, 183
  Porcelain Axe 121
  Porcelain Bottle 146, 186
  Porcelain Claw 122
  Porcelain Dish 133
  Roman 113
  Rose 63, 73, 74, 75
  Sinceny (France) 127
  Three Bells 122
  Three Golden Ash Barrels 23
  Two Boats 22
  Two Little Ships 97, 162
  Two Wild Men 74
  Urbino 1, 10
  Vincennes 156
  White Star 57, 122, 125
  Young Moor's Head 32, 37, 47, 51, 75, 99
faience 7, 9, 10, 17 and passim
  decline of 132
  Dutch 1, 2, 3, 4, 5, 6, 8, 17 and passim
  French 8, 105
  high-temperature 17, 73, 74, 129
  low-temperature 75
Faenza 4
  'bianchi di' 48, 50
famille verte: see Kangxi
famille rose 113
fan 123
  branches of 21
  having shape of 18; see also vases, tulip
Far East 10, 19, 20-2, 23, 25-6, 32, 38, 72, 74, 80, 104, 117, 122, 125
feather 150
fences 98, 100
  pagoda 101
festoons 70
Fétis 7
Fichelaar, Freevk Jane 180
fillet 86
firing 17, 18
  high-temperature 24
  low-temperature 23
  muffle- 23
five-colour ware 24
flash, rectangular 17
fleurons 73, 83, 109, 110
  double band of 19
  stylized 116
  tulip-shaped 72
Florence 9
flowers 7, 10, 18, 19, 21, 21, 24, 26, 68, 84, 85
  anemones 20
  carnations (black) 129
  chrysanthemums 75
  cut 25
  fantastic 79
  fleur-de-lis 8, 67, 109
  eight-petalled 31
  hearts of 81
  imaginary 152
  in reserve 86
  lotus 25
  roses 20
  yellow 129
  scatter of 72, 73, 75, 76
  sprays of 24, 74, 75, 87, 94, 103
  stems of 22, 99
  stylized 19, 121
  tulips 10, 20
  wreath of 20
flux 18, 24
Fo, dog of 51
folk ware 121
foliage, stylized 18, 31
fontage head-dress 73, 82
fountain and basin set 139
Frankfurt 71
frames
  plain 88-9
  rectangular 22
  well-defined 128
France/French 7, 22, 65, 130
  cavalrymen 7
  market 73

'stitch': see lambrequins
friezes 30, 31, 68, 73
  of floral scrolls 22
  of little angles 73
  of raised fleurons 10
  of tulip stems 22
  palmette 101
  superposed 37
fringes 22
Frijtom: see Frÿtom
Frisian ware 10
Frisius, Simon 24
fruit 10, 17
  grapes 9
  pomegranates 9; see also baskets and bowls
Frÿtom, Frederik van 9, 11, 12, 14, 21, 23, 34, 35, 38, 170
furnishings 22
  cradles 152
  tables 75, 82, 100

Gaal, Jan 162
Galestruzzi, Giovanni-Battista 24, 40
garniture sets 26, 30, 31, 38, 56, 73, 77, 94, 103
Gasnault 7
Gelder, Van 25
Genoa 9
Germany 18
gilding 23, 38, 114
  discreet 102
glass, painted 24
glaze 10, 17, 16, 18, 24, 73, 101, 122
  bluish tinge in 22
  coloured 75
  Dutch 1
  high-temperature 24
  in black 75, 93, 95, 97
  in white 93
  lead 5, 13, 17, 18, 29
  over- 18, 75
  under- 74
glazer 17
globes 118
Goethals, Jean Georges 33
gold 18, 23, 75-6, 111, 112
  litharge of; see also lead, oxide of
Goltzius, Hendrick 23, 112
gourd, double 26
  spouted 22
Goyen, Van 10
Grand Pensionary of the Nederlands 19
green 3, 10, 17, 18, 24, 74, 74, 76, 77, 80, 95, 97, 100, 110
  aka-e type 18
  emerald 75, 85, 100, 112
  olive- 81
greever: see glazer
grey 24, 110, 112
grisaille 113
Groelant, Jan 23
grotesque, Italian 1, 10
grounds 64
  black 69, 75, 92, 93, 95, 97, 98, 100, 101, 122
  bleu d'empoi 3, 4
  bleu persan 4
  blue 3, 4, 68, 124
  brown 75
  'chestnut' 126
  'chocolate' 75, 101, 122
  green 122
  grey-blue 126
  half-blue 58, 122
  'olive' 75, 99, 101
  red-scaled 80
  smaltino 4
Guérard 7
guilds (trade) 8, 19-21
  Butcher's 161
  dean of 22
  of St. Luke 19, 148

Haarlem 9, 10, 19, 176, 180
Hague, The 7
hair 84
Hamme, John Ariens van 182
Hampton Court, Water (or Queen's) Gallery 22-3, 26, 26, 27, 28
Hanau 71
handles 5, 15, 25-6, 31, 63
  brush 26
  convoluted 123
  in form of animal heads 103
  in form of chimeras 25
  knife and fork 76, 117
  plaited 74
  square 104
Hausmaler 18; see also painters; on glass
Havard, Henry 7, 7, 17, 19, 70, 74, 99, 132, 156
head-dresses: see fontange
hearts 150
  motif 121-2, 124, 126
  ruyi-sceptre 21
hedges 75, 75
  flowering 75, 142
Heukensfeldt-Jansen, M.A. 33
Helbig, J. 7, 21, 23-4, 26, 53, 74, 99, 125, 137
Hey, Reinier 35
high-temperature (grand feu): see firing and polychrome
Hoeve, Van der
  family 156 f
Honthorst 10
hooks 72
  in reserve 19
Honey, W.B. 26, 81
Hoppesteyn
  family 24-5, 75
  Jacob Wemmerz 23
  Rochus Jacobsz 23, 24, 75, 99
Hudig, Ferrand 9, 10, 21, 24, 132, 139, 176
human
  busts 69, 123
  figures 4
    acrobats 73
    actors 65
    beauties 106
    boys 88-9
    child dancing 91
    children (playing) 75, 78, 102
    Chinamen 37, 90, 136
    dignitary walking 17
    female 20, 88-9
    fishermen 147
    girl dancing 99
    hunters 43, 157, 169
    ladies (round faced) 91; see also 'slender ladies'
    madonnas 5
    monarchs 121
    mountebanks 65
    musicians 25, 100
    pedlars 71, 145
    plumed 22
    potters (in action) 10
    riders 73, 97
    royalty 17
    servants 19; see also Negroes
    tradesmen 73
  figurines 162, 163, 168
  heads
    girls 170
    masks 150
    monster 170
humorous motif 116
Huybrechtsz, Cornelis 21

Imari ware 75, 85, 87, 94, 96, 104, 108, 109
initials: see marks
inkstands 76
inscription, religious 10
interiors 25, 73
  church 14, 21

199

Far Eastern 91
interlace 17, 24
iron 17; see also red
Italy 1, 2, 4, 5, 7, 7, 9, 10, 10, 17, 18, 19, 20, 21, 26
Iznik
   'tomato red' 83

Japan/Japanese 18, 20, 21, 75, 91, 94, 104
jars
   albarello 123
   apothecaries' (or pharmacist's) 15, 136, 148
   lidded 22, 77, 91, 101
   spice 25
   syrup 123, 148
   tobacco 114, 138
Jonge, C.H. de 9, 22, 24-5, 73, 99, 105, 122
Jordaens, Jacobis 21
Jourde 7
jugs 21, 39, 63, 126, 131
   flat-handled 121
   handled 25
   puzzle 123, 130
   water 121
junk, clog-shaped 104

Kakiemon, family 75
Kam, Gerrit Pietersz 23
Kan, Lampet 148
Kangxi decoration: see blue-and-white
   biscuit wares 75
   famille verte ware 74, 84, 86
   style 22-3, 74, 91
kannetje: see jugs, handled
Kastels, de 26
Kerckhoff, Johan van 179, 180
kettles 123
key-fret motif 125
Keyser, Aelbrecht Cornelisz 22
Kherbeetje 7
Kiell, Albertus 122, 125
kiln, muffle 18, 130
knobs 123
   fruit-shaped 143
   on neck 79
   round 26
   spherical 36
   colouring of 102
Kocks, Adriaen 20, 21, 21, 22, 23-4, 24, 26, 74
   Pieter Adriaensz 29, 74, 103, 104, 109, 110
Kruyck, Gÿsbrecht (or Gijsbrecht) Lambrechtsz 23
kwaart: see glaze, lead

Laan, Jan van der 23, 121, 152
lacquer, imitation of: see painting
La Hogue, Battle of (Normandy) 35
lambrequins 20, 22, 36, 74, 74, 77, 79, 111
   lacey 74
   pompon 96
   scroll 96
   swag 96
landscapes 9, 12, 14, 21-2, 24, 121, 123, 132
   Chinese 98
   European 139
   fantastic 74, 77
   figured 37
   imaginary 11, 128
   night 98
   rocky 66
Lane, Arthur 7, 22, 26, 40, 45
lange lijsen: see 'slender ladies'
Law's system, collapse of 154
lead, oxide of 17-18; see also gold, litharge of
leaves 80, 101
   and flowers 20
   banana 23
   celery 123
   heather 72
   lettuce 123

star-shaped, group of 17
water-lily 126
legends 22
Lelong, Isaac 18
lids 25, 27, 28, 91, 101, 104, 113
   domed 26, 30, 36
   pewter 25
   tapered 73
light effects 24
lightning 150
   motif 76, 121, 122
Lille 17
Lion-Goldschmidt, Daisy 18, 20, 25, 75
Liverani, Giuseppe 75
Loenen 11
Loudon, John 7
Louis XIV 19
Löwenfinek, Adam Friedrich von 86
Lyons 9

majolica 9, 26
   Dutch 9, 24, 176
   Italian 18
Makkum 6, 180
Mander, Carel van 9
Mandl 7
manganese 15, 16, 17, 29, 32, 81; see also brown, purple
mannerist style 88-9
Mark, Saint, gospel of 14
marks 20, 23, 25, 112, 121, 122
   A.K. 18-21, 22, 22-4, 24, 27-8, 44-5, 182-3
   A.R. 65, 73, 76, 107, 116, 126
   C.H. 7, 21
   C.L. 21
   C.W. 67
   D.A.W. 131
   Dex 138
   D.L.V.H. 132
   D.P.A.W. 122
   Fortune 122
   F.V. Frÿtom 9
   G.K. 23, 73, 76
   I.R. 8
   I.V.D. 75, 99
   I.V.H. 73
   I.V.L. 23, 124, 152
   I.W. 36, 38, 40, 41, 42, 43
   J.B. + star 70
   K.V.D.K. 123
   K.V.K. 123
   L.V.E. 71, 72, 74, 74, 79, 80, 93, 101, 125
   P.A.K. 29, 74, 75, 76, 103-6, 109-10, 112
   R. 63, 66
   R.I.H.S. 37, 39
   Roos 62, 75
   Sophia de Nane 121
   Star 57
   S.V.E. 15-17, 22
   Van Duyn 133
   William 19
   W.R. 56, 77, 91, 106, 111, 122
Marot Daniel 22, 24, 25, 26, 45, 70, 74, 112, 156, 170
Mary of Burgundy 9
mascarons
   bearded heads of 74
   mouth of 123
masters: see potters; master faience
mastic 17
mauve 112
   pale 88-9
medallion 1, 10, 25, 70, 121, 126
   oval 92
   round 13, 75, 86
Meissen, porcelain factory 117, 130, 150
   dishes 108
   figurines 82
   turquoise decorations 122
metalwork 78, 79, 105, 107, 123
Meulen, Van der 121, 121
Middle Ages 24

Milan 9
Milde, Ary-Jansz de 25, 52
mina'i wares 18
Ming, dynasty 5, 10, 91
   style 26
miniature style 77, 85, 92
'mixed technique' 18, 23, 24, 31, 111
monochrome 23
monograms: see marks
monsters, gaping 27, 28
   human-headed 86
   salmon-tinted 103
Montagne 7
moon 98
moulds 76
Muller, Jean 2
Museums:
   Amsterdam, Rijksmuseum 7, 9, 11, 14, 16, 21, 22, 23-4, 25, 33, 37, 41-2, 74, 83-4, 86, 101, 114, 116, 139, 175
      Loudon Collection 14, 58, 112, 129
   Arnhem, Gemeente Museum 25, 122
   Brussels, Musées royaux d'Art et d'Histoire 7, 7, 8, 10, 12, 15, 21, 22, 26, 72, 97, 131, 137, 156
      Evenepöel Collection 8, 12, 38, 39, 47, 69, 97, 133, 160, 168
      Gustave Vermeersch Collection 100
   Delft, Stedelijk Museum 'Het Prinsenhof' 57, 95, 123
   Douai, Musée de la Chartreuse 23
   The Hague, Gemeente Museum 7, 19, 32, 51, 61, 62, 78, 104
      Van der Burgh Collection 71, 138, 140
   Leeuwarden, 'Het Princessehof' 105
   Lille, Musée des Beaux-Arts 76
      Van der Straten Donation 107
      Vicq Donation 102
   Limoges, Musée national Adrien Dubouché 21, 33, 66, 150
      Gasnault Collection 21, 49, 67, 68, 99, 105, 146
   London, British Museum 34, 40, 53, 120
      Victoria and Albert Museum 20, 22, 25, 31, 45, 73, 75, 76, 81, 93, 150
   Paris, Musée Carnavalet 121
      Musée des Arts décoratifs 29, 64, 72, 79, 87, 91, 115, 117, 123, 127, 132, 142
   Private collections 92, 99, 103, 109, 128, 155
   Rotterdam, Boymans van Beuningen Museum 3, 86
   Rouen, Musée des Beaux-Arts 11
   Sèvres, Musée National de Céramique 1-6, 15, 17-18, 20, 25, 30, 35, 38, 43, 45, 46, 48, 52, 54-5, 60, 65, 70, 75, 77, 80, 82, 94, 96, 98, 108-9, 113, 118, 122-3, 125, 128, 130, 135
      Chompret Bequest 1, 3, 134
      Fombeure Bequest 148
      Grémiou Donation 126
      J. Duval Donation 17
      Landeau Donation 174
      Moulard Donation 109
      Papillon Bequest 109
      Petitet Donation 106, 152
      Viefville Bequest 18, 56
mythological subjects 2, 5, 10, 23
   'The Loves of Venus and Mercury' 2

Nantes, Edict of 22
Near East 16, 18, 19
neck 79, 101, 113 and *passim*
   perforated 130
Negroes 75, 82, 114, 155
   heads of 25
nests 155, 158
Neurdenburg, E. 21
Nevers 4, 122
Niculoso, Francesco 9
Noothoven, J.-M. 180

obelisk 76
   four-sided 27
   table ornaments 102; see also vases, tulip
ochre, red: see red slip
'old Japan' 75
orange 10, 74
   -red 89
   -yellow 1, 3, 46, 47, 77
Ottema, Nanne 180
oxides, metal 18

Paape, Gerrit 17, 18, 186
pagodas 25, 79, 93, 96, 98, 101, 102, 142
painters 19, 21, 100
   Chapelle 82
   delftware 19, 21, 31, 37
   flower 24
   Italian 38; see also miniature style painting 9, 66, 77, 83, 102
   Dutch 14, 68, 85
   Flemish 10
   on glass 18, 24
   portraits, of Louis XV 68
   of pastors 33, 38
   painted on plaques 33
Palamede 23
Palm Sunday 13
palisade 94, 128
palmettes 72, 100, 101
pan, conical cream 22
   cream 76
panels 19, 21, 108
   'lotus' 32, 118
   rib-separated 77
   scrolled 147
pannekoekjes: see dishes without rim
Pannier 7
panther 74
parasol 17
Pascal 7
paving
   in perspective 64
peacocks
   feather pattern 121
   tail (or fan) motif 156; see also animals; birds
pedestals 103
   rectangular 18
Peelen, Ida 22
pegs 18
pendentives 22, 36, 41-3
pen-holder 118
period, classical 13 and *passim*
Persia, art of 4
perspective 14
petit feu: see firing; low-temperature
phoenixes 74, 86, 100, 101
Piccardt, Henricus Arnoldus 186
Piccolpasso, Cipriano 9
pig, butchered 26
Pijnacker, Adriaen 74
pine cones 126
pink 24, 75, 100, 112
plants 11, 36, 81
   acanthus 132, 133
   exotic 17
   'fishbone'-shaped 23
   marsh 72
   traditional 95
   water 91
plaques 9, 11, 12, 22, 23, 22-4, 88-9
   octagonal 14, 21
   ornamental 6, 10, 121
   kermess 8, 21
   oval 24, 35, 88-9, 100
   rectangular 8, 11, 21, 33-4, 46-7, 90
   square 25, 64
   with foliate border 49
plateelbakker: see potter, master faience
plates
   little 18
   rough clay 17; see also dishes
'playing card' motifs 122

plinth *28, 102,* 180
  central 22
polychrome 10, 18, *18,* 23-4, *65,* 74, 75, *97, 99, 124*
  enamels *113,* 115-16
  high-temperature *1, 2, 3, 4, 5,* 24, *46, 47, 48, 51, 56, 57, 63, 65,* 74, *77, 79, 80, 81, 82, 83, 84, 85, 86, 100, 122, 123,* 127-9
porcelain 10, 17, 20, 76
  Chinese 18, *29*
  'first Dutch' 10
  English *108*
  French *117*
  Japanese 75
  Jesuit ware *115*
  kraak 20
  works 18
'porcellanous' effect *13*
porringers *10, 130*
  lidded *104*
  two-handled *5*
Portugal 20
potash 17
potiche: *see* vase; lidded
Poterat, Louis *183*
potters, master faience 19, 20, 23, 24, *112*
  jury of 19
pottery, Islamic 18
potting families 19
'Precious Objects' (Eight) *77, 115, 121*
pricked drawings: *see* stencils
pricking *11*
printers 19
prints 23
  'months of the year' *121*
profile
  conical *95*
  scalloped 25
  swelling *37*
'pugging': *see* clay; kneading
purple *3,* 17, 22, 24, *32,* 75, *84, 94, 102,* 122
  aubergine- *155*
  bluish 17; *see also* trek
pyramids 26, *28*

quartering 10
Queborn, Crispijn van 23, *33,*

'radiating style' *80*
'Rape of Europa' (Rijksmuseum) 76, *112*
Raphael *1,* 10, 23, 156
red 17, 18, 24, 74, 75, *80, 95, 96, 115*
  and blue *80*
  from gold 18
  iron 75, *113*
  slip 16
  tomato- *83*
Reformation 9
Reijgersbergen, Augustyn van 74, *183*
Révérend, A. 74
  Claude *183*
Rex, William 22; *see also* marks (W.R.)
Rijsselberg, Ary van *116*
rijsttafelstel 25, *41, 57, 123, 125*
rims *2,* 7, 10, *12, 13,* 21, *70, 72, 72,* 73, 74, *75, 84, 85, 90, 109, 110, 137*
  flanged 25
  flaring *114*
  flat *10, 49,* 74, *80, 81, 86*

rocks *32, 81, 96*
  'perforated' *17, 75, 76, 79,* 87-9, *94, 95, 103, 104, 144*
rococo elements *129, 130, 139, 140, 144*
Romano, Giulio 23
  tapestry cartoons of *38*
Rome 9
'room', 'French style' 22
rosettes 10, 23, *126,* 150
Rotterdam 9
'rotting': *see* clay; weathering
Rouen 9, *82, 105, 122, 127*
  designs 74
  dishes *84*
  lambrequins at 74
  two-colour effect *80*
  wares *81*
Roullier 7
ruyi sceptre *29, 37, 39, 123*
Ryswick, Treaty of 150

saggars 18
Salin, Patrice 7
salt-cellar 20
'sampler design' *121*
sand 17, 18
Sanderus, Lambertus *122*
sauce boat 76
saucers 25
Savino, Guido da 9
Savona 9, 25
Saxony 18
Sazerac de Forges 7
scabbard, makers of 19
scenes
  battle 7
  Chinese *15,* 22, 23
  genre 22, *63*
  kermess *8,* 10, 21
  life of Constantine *38*
  musical *63*
  pastoral 122, *129, 172*
  rural *63*
screens *84*
scrolls 22, 24, *72,* 74, *112, 132*
  belt of *37*
  birds in *68*
  flower *10, 30*
  frieze of *37, 39*
  lacey *69*
  in reserve *129*
sculptors 19
seascapes *73, 121*
seasons, symbolized *20*
Serlio, Sebastiano 25
Seven United Provinces *7,* 9, 10
Seville 9
Sèvres 122
shareholders 21, 74, *121, 142,* 150, *154*
shells 76, *84, 112*
ships, Chinese and European *35*
shoulder *77, 94, 101, 113*
shrubs: *see* bushes
signatures
  I Altubon *35*
  Rit Reinier *35; see also* marks
signs
  crescent *8*
  water *79, 121, 122*
Sino-Japanese *78, 106, 142*

sledges *147*
'slender ladies' (*meiren*) 75, *82, 84, 105,* 170
smalt 17; *see also* grounds; blue
smaltino: *see* grounds
soda 17
Song, period 18
South Sea bubble *154*
Spain 9, 10, *19*
sphinxes 25
spirals 10, *79*
  blue *80, 94*
spittoon *138*
  with handle *114*
sponged technique *66*
spouts 22
  angled 76
  rectangular *95, 142*
Spranger, Bartholomeus *2*
stand, footed 76
stars 10
stencils 17, *49, 111, 134, 172*
stoneware, red 18, 25, 75
straets goet 10
stripes, blue and green *92*
sun 76
  of St Bernardin *107*
sylphids 22
système rayonnant: *see* radiating style

tables *82; see also* furniture
tassels 22, *64*
tea 25, *78*
tea caddies *17,* 22, 25, *44,* 92-3
  neck of 26
  rectangular or square 26, *92*
  little *93*
teapots 18, 25, *52, 78, 99, 127*
  crowned 25
  globular 25
  little *99*
  on stand *78*
  red stoneware 18, 25, *52, 78*
  with conical spouts 25
  with flattened profile *78*
terrace 88-9
Teniers, David 10, *60*
themes, Chinese 31
  Italian *15*
  oriental 74
  Turkish *83*
Thornhill, Sir James *119*
three-colour ware 24
thrower (*de draaier*) 17, 19
tiles 10, 21, *176 f*
tilemaker 19
tin ash (oxide) 17
trees *29, 98*
  trunks *85*
trek *13,* 17, *20,* 22-3, *28, 66, 118*
trellises *72, 115*
Triple Alliance, the 19
tripod *63, 108*
trompe-l'œil decoration *122, 123*
Tulk, Adolf *186*
tureens 25, *140,* 155
  oval *123*
  small *104*
  with lid and tray *143*
Turner, Donald *186*
two-colour decoration *93*

Udine, Giovanni da *1*
unicorn *86, 146*
United Province: *see* Seven United Provinces

Valckenhoff, Cornelis H. 21
Van Queborn 23
vases 16, 18, *18,* 20, 22, 25-6, *26, 27, 28, 31, 36, 38,* 54-6, *60,* 87, *90, 101, 103, 106, 108, 125,* 182
  baluster *26, 31, 36, 81*
  beaker-shaped *26*
  Chinese *56, 63*
  fan-shaped (tulip) *26, 103*
  flared *56*
  footed 25
  for sets 22
  lidded *26, 36, 73, 80, 113*
  lobed body *29*
  hemispherical 26
  monumental (at Hampton Court) 22, *26*
  pagoda *182*
  shaped like sledges *123*
  spouted *160*
  tulip *18,* 25-6, *26, 27, 28, 54, 55, 103*
  waisted *146; see also* handles
Vecht, A. 11, 21
Venice *4,* 9, 10, 18
Verhaast, Gÿsbrecht (or Gijsbrecht) Claesz 24, *46, 47, 170*
Verstelle, Geertruy *130*
Verstraeten, Willem Jansz 10
Victorsz (or Fictorsz), Louwÿs *71,* 74
Vitruvius 26
violin 155-6, *164, 165*
volute *30, 63, 112*
Voskuil-Groenewegen, S.M. *140*
Vroom, Henrich 9

Walle, Jacobus van de *182*
Wanli period *17,* 22-3, *36, 71,* 74
warmer 76
  tripod *78*
Weigert, Roger 22
Westphalia, Treaty of 9, *19*
wheel, potter's 17
white *12,* 16, 18, *21, 64*
  brilliant *29*
  opaque (barium) *4*
'white on white' *134*
wig stands 26
William III (of Orange) 19, 22, *28, 48, 182*
  V (of Orange) 150, *186*
  and Mary *25, 26, 27*
willow, stylized *77*
wit 17; *see also* white
Witt, Jan de 19
winkelhouder: *see* shareholders
wreaths *109*
  of laurel 22
  oval *80*
Wÿtmans (or Wijtmans), Claesz Jansz 10

yellow 10, 17, 24, 74, *74,* 75, *81*-3, *86, 95, 96, 97*
  dotted with red *85*
  golden- *77, 93, 101*
  high-temperature *101*

Zodiac, signs of *115,* 121

Printed in Switzerland

RECEIVED MAR 3 1 1983 $45.00

FOUREST, HENRY PIERRE 09/18/86
DELFTWARE: FAIENCE \N AT DELFT
(8) 1980 R738.37 FOU
0652 01 491106 01 1 (IC=2)

B065201491106011B

South Huntington Public Library
Huntington Station, New York
11746

005